PLANNING A WEDDING
THE WEDDING PLANNER WAY

PLANNING A WEDDING THE WEDDING PLANNER WAY

Over a decade of experience in one book to make sure your wedding day goes with only the one hitch.

HAZEL WALSHAW

Content copyright © Hazel Walshaw, 2019

All rights reserved. No portion of this book may be reproduced, stored in a retrieval system or transmitted at any time or by any means mechanical, electronic, photocopying, recording or otherwise, without the prior, written permission of the author.

The right of Hazel Walshaw to be identified as the author of this work has been asserted by her in accordance with the Copyright, Designs and Patents act 1988.

First printed 2019

DEDICATION

This book is dedicated to all the wonderful couples who allowed me to be part of their special day, and to my husband, Neil, for making my wedding...er...OUR wedding amazing and even learning the cha-cha-cha for the first dance, despite hating any formal dancing. That's love right there.

CONTENTS

About the Author   Pg 5
Introduction   Pg 7

Section 1: 6-12 months before 'I do'

Chapter 1:	Ceremonies	Pg 13
Chapter 2:	Finding your Wedding Style	Pg 21
Chapter 3:	Venues	Pg 25
Chapter 4:	Catering	Pg 33
Chapter 5:	Bar Hire and Drinks	Pg 43
Chapter 6:	Decorations and Flowers	Pg 51
Chapter 7:	Photography	Pg 61
Chapter 8:	Videography	Pg 67
Chapter 9:	The Wedding Cake	Pg 73
Chapter 10:	Entertaining your Guests	Pg 81
Chapter 11:	Transport	Pg 85
Chapter 12:	Wedding Attire	Pg 91
Chapter 13:	Hair and Make-up	Pg 101

Section 2: 2-6 months before 'I do'

Chapter 14:	Stationery	Pg 109
Chapter 15:	Preparing the Seating Plan	Pg 113

Chapter 16:	Wedding Traditions	Pg 117
Chapter 17:	The Speeches	Pg 123
Chapter 18:	Children at Weddings	Pg 126
Chapter 19:	Personalising your Wedding	Pg 129

Section 3: 1 month before 'I do'

Chapter 20:	The Final Weeks	Pg 135
Chapter 21:	The Wedding Day	Pg 139
Chapter 22:	Final Thoughts from the Wedding Planner	Pg 145
Acknowledgements		Pg 147
Contributors		Pg 149
Appendix 1:	Checklists	Pg 151

ABOUT THE AUTHOR

I have spent over ten exciting, challenging, rewarding, sometimes stressful, but joyful years as a wedding planner in Yorkshire with my own business, Love To Marry Wedding Planning. In that time, I planned and coordinated many different weddings from hotels, marquees, stately homes, village halls and castles.

There were expensive weddings and budget-conscious weddings. Religious weddings with over 800 guests in the city, to humanist ceremonies and chilled out celebrations in the countryside.

I specialised in the unusual and quirky. One of my more memorable weddings was a punk-rock wedding in abbey ruins with dry ice, music and lights, which was featured in Rock n Roll Bride's blog.

I also know not every couple wants, or can afford, a wedding planner, or an on-the-day coordinator. So, this book will give you the experience of a wedding planner at your fingertips for a fraction of the cost. I hope that my years of experience and wedding day anecdotes will help you have a memorable, stress-free and hopefully glitch-free day.

I live in Leeds with my husband, Neil, our three boys and our three-legged Siberian husky, Skye.

For more wedding-related information, subscribe to my YouTube channel, Weddings and Tarot Love, visit my website at www.hazelwalshaw.co.uk or contact me on hazel@lovetomarry.co.uk. Follow me on Instagram: Hazel_Bouquets and Hazel_Walshaw or Facebook: Love To Marry or even Twitter: @HazelWalshaw.

"Hazel, I wanted to write and tell you that we decided that the best thing about our whole wedding day was YOU! You *made* the whole of the evening reception. It all just flowed, and we were soooo happy to have you there organising and sorting things out. Just knowing you were in charge made us not have to think about anything stressful. You sorted out the glitches (oops, I found the missing place cards at home!) and you thought of things and sorted them out before they even became a problem. All the suppliers knew exactly what to do, and when, and where, and you whipped the whole event into the shape I wanted it! The venue looked AMAZING, from the sparkley lights and trees at the door, to the tables, candles and the cake of cheese inside! It truly would not have been the fabulous success it was, without your guiding hand, advice, and hard work." **Liza and Dan**

"Hazel is an absolute legend. We gave her a very vague brief with lots of very unusual ideas, and she created the single most amazing wedding in history!! She even managed to be everywhere at once on the wedding day (some kind of wedding planner magic no doubt!!) We never had to look for her, she was always there at the right time grinning her head off. We could never have had such a wonderful wedding without her. Hazel, we really can't thank you enough for making our punk rock wedding the most fantastic night for us and our guests. You rock!!" **Rachel and Dale**

INTRODUCTION

"It is a truth universally acknowledged, that a single man in possession of a good fortune, must be in want of a wife." - Jane Austen, Pride and Prejudice

A lot of time and money goes into planning a wedding, whether your own or someone else's. You want to make sure that the day itself reflects all the hard work you have put in. There are so many different things to think about, order, organise, create, and hire that it can be easy to miss something. You don't want to realise you have forgotten something on the day.

As a wedding planner for over ten years, I have planned and coordinated many different weddings, and in that time, I have learnt a lot of lessons. You can't know it all when you start out and each wedding over those first few years was a steep learning curve. Each wedding gave me more items to add to my list of questions to ask the couple or the suppliers, and things to make sure are taken care of. Unless you are a wedding planner, you won't be able to 'get it right next time', so you need to get it right this time.

This book will give you plenty to think about and will include real-life situations so you can see what could and did go wrong, how it was fixed, or what lessons were learnt for the next wedding. You will also find out what goes on behind-the-scenes, as the couple and guests enjoy the wedding day. The role of a wedding planner is not an easy one. It requires quick decision making and plenty of stamina as I would be on my feet ALL day! I once wore a tracker and found that I had walked over 5km. That was just around a marquee!

If I gave you only one piece of advice in this book, it would be **Don't Make Assumptions!** - Never assume your partner/family member/supplier knows what you are wanting if you haven't told them. Maybe **Communicate** should be high up on that list too! I've planned weddings where the bride rarely responded to any of the emails I sent with ideas or options. I would have to ask two or three times over a month, only to end up getting an answer saying she had sorted it! It's hard to plan a wedding when there is no communication. Suppliers are waiting for replies and the poor planner (if you have one) is stuck in the middle! If you have a wedding planner helping you, do communicate regularly. If they send you something you are not keen on, tell them. They need to know what you don't like as much as what you do like. Same with your partner. Communicate and make sure they are involved throughout. Compromise where necessary.

Who is this book for?

This book is for anyone planning a wedding* in the UK, regardless of budget, who does not have the expertise of a wedding planner to hand. This book will cover all the elements of planning a wedding, but it is specifically aimed at couples getting married in locations that are not hotels, stately homes, banqueting halls, castles or where all the wedding expertise and catering is on hand and included with the venue. That's not to say there won't be useful information for other types of venues. I got married in a zoo and that included all the furniture, catering, drinks packages, etc., but what it didn't seem to include was someone to make sure all the suppliers were there (or could even get into the venue!), or a cake knife was put out, for example. We had to stand around by the cake for ten minutes while someone searched the venue for a member of staff to get one. This book is also useful for any budding wedding planners as I will detail the approaches I would take when planning and coordinating weddings.

When I say 'wedding', I include civil ceremonies, civil partnerships, religious and humanist marriages, etc.

How is the book set out?

This book starts with the big items and works through to the details, in the order you need to focus on them, and finishes with the wedding day itself. This is set out over three sections. The first covers twelve to six months before the wedding day and goes through all the main suppliers or vendors you might need to hire. The second section covers six to two months before the wedding day and will look at personalising your wedding day, traditions, the seating plan, speeches, etc. The third section covers two months up to the wedding day itself. So, this will include the final weeks leading up to the wedding day, creating a wedding day timetable and what to expect on the day itself. As this is planning the wedding planner way, there will be some topics that won't be covered in this book such as hen or stag dos, as they are typically organised by the couple or their friends. I also was not involved with destination weddings, so these won't be covered either.

Each chapter will give an overview of the main options and the differences between them. I will also touch on budgets and give an idea of which options are usually lower cost than others. I will give examples from real-life weddings and situations to look out for or be aware of. At the back of the book will be some useful check lists.

SECTION 1

6-12 MONTHS BEFORE 'I DO'

CHAPTER 1
CEREMONIES

"The real act of marriage takes place in the heart, not in the ballroom or church or synagogue. It's a choice you make—not just on your wedding day, but over and over again—and that choice is reflected in the way you treat your husband or wife." – Barbara de Angelis

What kind of wedding are you having? Are you following the traditions of your religion? If you are religious, then the chances are your wedding ceremony will be in your local place of worship. If you are not religious, you can opt for a civil ceremony or a humanist service at a location of your choice.

Currently (2019) in England and Wales, the venue has the marriage licence. So, if you have got your heart set on a ceremony on a hill or an unlicensed location, you will need to do the legal bit beforehand. In Scotland and Northern Ireland, the law is a bit different, so it is always best to check with your local Registry Office before you plan your wedding somewhere unusual.

Ceremony Options

Religious Ceremonies

A religious ceremony takes place at any registered religious building. The marriage needs to be registered by an authorised person, such as a minister, immediately after the ceremony. You will need to check the venue has an authorised person, otherwise, you will need to book a registrar. The majority of religions are licenced to conduct a religious wedding ceremony, which is also legally binding. Some faiths may require a civil ceremony to ensure you are legally married. Couples are often asked to attend weekly services for a set time before getting married at a religious venue.

Civil Ceremonies

A civil ceremony is a non-religious ceremony conducted by a registrar in a registry office or a licenced wedding venue. There is usually limited scope for personalisation such as the wedding vows, but you can have readings and songs, as long as they have no religious content. There are many venues licenced for civil ceremonies, from town halls and hotels to country halls and castles. More unusual venues may be licenced, such as zoological gardens, historical sites and art galleries. You will be able to find a list on your local council website.

Humanist Ceremonies

According to the humanism.org.uk website, these ceremonies give you the opportunity to marry where you want, when you want and how you want.

A humanist celebrant will write the ceremony tailored specifically for each couple and can help you write your own vows. These ceremonies are not legally binding in England, Wales, Guernsey or the Isle of Man at this moment in time, and therefore, you will need to perform the legal bit beforehand, or afterwards. Some couples may do this with just a couple of witnesses, then have the humanist ceremony as the main event the guests attend, and some couples make both ceremonies part of the celebration. Humanist ceremonies are recognised in Scotland and Northern Ireland. Visit www.humanism.org.uk/ceremonies/non-religious-weddings/ to find out more.

Same-Sex Weddings

These weddings are recognised in England, Scotland and Wales, but not Northern Ireland. Civil partnerships are recognised in all areas of the UK. These give same-sex couples the same legal rights as a heterosexual married couple with respect to pension rights, next-of-kin, etc. but there are also differences. https://www.gov.uk/government/publications/comparison-of-civil-partnership-and-marriage-for-same-sex-couples website has more information.

Outdoor weddings

In England and Wales, you can get married outdoors as long as the ceremony takes place under a fixed structure and that structure is licenced. So, think arbours and gazebos at licenced venues.

I coordinated a number of outdoor ceremonies. For some of them, the couples had legally got married beforehand elsewhere and then had a ceremony outside which the guests attended as the main ceremony. One couple had their wedding at a licenced barn and they opened up the large side doors. The guests sat outside, the bride walked up the outside aisle and the couple stood in the doorway to get married by the registrar - so as close to being outside as possible. This had the added benefit that if it rained, we could just move the chairs inside and set up there instead.

In Scotland, the law is different. You can get married anywhere as long as a Minister or celebrant is present. The venue does not have to be approved or licenced.

Where can ceremonies be held?

According to the citizensadvice.org.uk website, the following is a list of places where a marriage can take place:

- A Registry office
- Premises approved by the local authority such as a hotel
- A church of the Church of England, Church in Wales, Church of Ireland, Presbyterian or Roman Catholic Church in N. Ireland
- A synagogue or any other private place if both partners are Jewish
- A Meeting House if one or both partners are either members of the Society of Friends (Quakers) or are associated with the Society by attending meetings
- Any registered religious building (England and Wales only)
- The home of one of the partners if the partner is housebound or

detained, for example, in prison

- A place where one partner is seriously ill and not expected to recover, for example, in hospital
- A licenced naval, military or air force chapel.

How to get married - the legalities

As mentioned, you can get married by a civil ceremony or a religious ceremony. In both cases, the following legal requirements must be met:

- The marriage must be conducted by a person or in the presence of a person authorised to register marriages in the district
- The marriage must be entered in the marriage register and signed by both parties, two witnesses, the person who conducted the ceremony and, if that person is not authorised to register marriages, the person who is registering the marriage.

Civil Ceremonies

On the Government website (www.gov.uk), it states: "You must decide where to have your marriage or civil partnership ceremony before 'giving notice'. To give notice, you will sign a legal statement at your local registry office saying you intend to get married or form a civil partnership. This must include details of the final venue for your ceremony. You must hold your ceremony within 12 months of 'giving notice'." Again, your local registry office will have all the information you need and you will be able to find details on your local council website.

In England and Wales, you must give a minimum of 28 day's notice before the marriage can take place and both partners must be resident for seven days before notice is given. There will be a fee for giving notice.

During a civil ceremony, each partner is required to repeat a standard set of promises which cannot be changed but may be added to as long as the additions are not religious.

You need to say the declaratory words:
I do solemnly declare that I know not of any lawful impediment why I [name] may not be joined in matrimony to [name].

You also need to say the contracting words which are the legal words that marry you and these feature towards the end of the ceremony:
I call upon these persons here present, to witness that I [name] do take thee [name] to be my lawful wedded wife/husband.

Additional words can be added before or after the contracting words to complete the wedding vows.

During a civil partnership, there are no legal words that need to be said, however, most ceremonies include the following paragraph:
I declare that I know not of any legal reason why we may not register as partners in law. I understand that on signing this document, we will be forming a civil partnership with each other.

Exchanging rings are not a legal requirement. After the ceremony, the marriage register is signed by both partners and the registrar. Two or more witnesses must also sign at the time of the marriage. Witnesses don't have to be a certain age but you should check with the person marrying you if they have an age limit on who they will accept. Witnesses must understand the language of the ceremony and have the mental capacity to understand what's taking place. Registry office staff are not allowed to act as witnesses.

Marriages in the Church of England and the Church in Wales

Instead of going to the Superintendent Registrar before the ceremony, banns (a notice of the proposed marriage) can be read in the parish church of each of the partners and in the church where it has been agreed the marriage can take place. Banns must be read on three Sundays before the ceremony.

In England, in some cases, the vicar may advise that you need to apply to the Church of England for a licence instead of using the banns procedure. You can find out more about getting married in the Church of England on the Church of England website at www.yourchurchwedding.org.

Visit the citizensadvice.org.uk website for more information on the different religious ceremony requirements.
https://www.citizensadvice.org.uk/family/living-together-marriage-and-civil-partnership/getting-married/)

Summary

- Decide on what type of ceremony you are having (Religious/Civil/Humanist)

- Book your Registrar/Celebrant/Religious ceremony
- Give notice at your local Registry office

CHAPTER 2
FINDING YOUR WEDDING STYLE

"Marriage is a wonderful invention: then again, so is a bicycle repair kit" - Billy Connolly

Have you looked through bridal magazines? Have you scoured Pinterest for hours on end? Have you been following the wedding trends of the young Royals or celebrities on Instagram? Of course you have!

Pick out the things you like - the colours, the vibe, the type of venue or location. A city wedding in a trendy hotel or art gallery will have a different vibe to a barn wedding in a field, miles from the nearest town. Do you want to feel glamorous and sophisticated? Then maybe sitting on a hay bale wearing colourful wellies isn't for you. I have known wedding planners who can't abide these style of weddings, and wouldn't know what to do with a hay bale if presented with one!

Do you both have a hobby that you share? Love travelling? Favourite destination? Into music? Love the circus? You can theme a wedding around most things. Once you have a theme in mind, you can then begin picking out the decor, attire, entertainment, etc., to fit the theme.

Venues will be discussed in the next chapter, but make sure you pick a venue that works for you and reflects your ethos. I got married in a zoo and we chose that over the other venues we had seen because a) it was interesting (never been to a wedding in a zoo before) and b) all the profits went to the zoo charity rather than to a hotel chain or private owner. When picking a venue or location, what places have great meaning for you both? Are you wanting an all-in-one venue or do you want a separate ceremony and reception venue? What about a destination wedding?

And remember, there are two of you celebrating this day so make sure you are both reflected in the style of the day. Got a partner who eats, breathes, and lives football? Then having a day that doesn't include even a small element of this is unfair to your partner. Even if you can't abide football or the clashing team colours!

Create a Mood Board

This is fun and you can create a physical board and cut out images and stick them onto a board, or you can have a virtual board and use a site like Pinterest to gather images you like. By gathering all the images you like together in one place, you will likely see a theme emerge. Are you collecting photos where everything is a particular colour? Are you picking winter wonderland wedding images? Maybe you'll prefer a December wedding over a summer one. So, have a look through all these images as a couple and work out what you **both** like.

If you are having a wedding planner or a venue stylist, this mood board will be invaluable at conveying the look of the wedding you are wanting.

Budget

What is your budget? According to Hitched.co.uk, the average wedding in the UK now costs £31,000. However, if the exceptionally high budgets

(£100,000 or more) and London-centric weighting is removed, then nationally, the average wedding is actually nearer £11,875 with 59% of couples spending between £5000 and £15,000 (guidesforbrides.co.uk). 50% of the budget is usually allocated to venue hire, catering and drinks, with 10% on the bridal gown and photography, and around 4-5% of the budget each on flowers, entertainment and ceremony costs. The rest of the remaining budget is split between menswear, cake and other costs.
https://www.guidesforbrides.co.uk/business-information/cost-of-weddings-uk

There are plenty of ways to splurge and save on your wedding day and it helps to find out what is most important to you, so you know where to spend your hard-earned (or possibly borrowed) pounds. For example, if you want as many guests as possible to celebrate and have a party, then maybe a cheap venue with cost-effective catering is where you could save. You could then splurge on a free bar and an amazing band. Or if you are foodies, you might want to splurge your money on the catering. There are many blogs and books for the budget-savvy bride. So, plenty of resources available online.

The one thing that is important is that you both agree on the budget and the spending priorities.

At the back of the book, I include some of the questions I used to ask couples during consultations to find out what was most important to them.

Summary

- Decide on location
- Decide on the number of venues
- Both agree on the budget and create a spreadsheet to keep track
- Agree on your spending priorities
- Gather images of things you like to create a wedding mood board
- Agree on a theme or style for your wedding

CHAPTER 3
VENUES

"Love recognizes no barriers. It jumps hurdles, leaps fences, penetrates walls to arrive at its destination full of hope." — Maya Angelou

The first big-ticket item is the venue. Without the venue booked, you can't book any other suppliers as they need to know the date and venue to get reliable quotes or to check availability. Do you set the date then find a venue that's available? Or do you find the venue and go with one of the dates they have available? Obviously, that depends if you have your heart set on a particular venue or if you need a particular date because it is special or fits in around work commitments, holidays or visiting family.

The venue also serves as the backdrop to your wedding day and the style of wedding, colours, catering, etc. will often be dictated around the venue choice. For example, if you have a Tee-pee style marquee in a field or garden, you are likely to prefer a more rustic-looking, relaxed wedding day. Getting married in a castle? You might go for a more classic wedding day.

Venue options

Venues like hotels, stately homes and some more unusual venues (castles, stadiums, zoological gardens, theatres, and ships, for example) often come with their own in-house wedding coordination team and caterers. These require less planning as they already have much of what you need. I'll mainly be focusing on the venues that are blank canvases and the main ones are listed below.

Marquees

These can come in a variety of styles. A traditional white frame marquee can be dressed to suit many styles from chic to country depending on the decorations you choose. Yurts and Tee-pee styles are very popular, and these often come with fire pits, long tables and bench seating and are perfect for a homely, laid back wedding day. You can also hire colourful Moroccan or Indian style tents. There are a lot of choices when it comes to marquees and tents, so it pays to do your research.

You do need somewhere to put a marquee though. So, you will need to have friends or family with a large flat field or garden, or you will need to hire a field or use the grounds of a wedding venue (costs can vary for the site hire).

The marquee company often work with particular hire companies or they have their own equipment available to hire. You will need to include a water source, flooring, generator, heating (even in summer), lighting and toilets when hiring a marquee. Even if it's in your garden - you won't want all your guests trooping in and out and queuing for your downstairs loo. Or worst still, blocking it.

This situation happened at one of the weddings I coordinated early on in my career. I did advise the couple and the brides' parents, who owned the house and garden, that they needed to hire toilets, but they assured me they didn't! If I had been more experienced, I might have been more persuasive. And a generator is a must. This same couple also decided they could run the electrics from their house supply. Twenty minutes before the guests returned from the church, the caterer blew the circuits and plunged the Moroccan tent into darkness, so don't skimp on these important elements! In case you were wondering, the situation was saved by one of the guests being an electrician and the problem was a burnt-out plug in the downstairs loo.

Marquees are not a cheap option as everything needs to be hired, including the tables and chairs, catering equipment and bar. By the time you have hired everything, you can spend as much or even more than a decent hotel or country house.

A checklist of useful questions to ask the marquee company can be found at the back of the book.

Village Halls and Function Rooms

Village halls, church halls or even a function room, are on the opposite of the venue cost scale and are the budget option for venue hire. However, they don't have to look cheap when decorated well (See chapter 4) and they leave you more money for other parts of the wedding. They usually have a small kitchen, a stage which is great for the band, and a car park. Some halls will have tables and chairs included, although these are often of the Formica long trestle table and folding chairs variety. So, if this isn't for you, you will need to hire these. I used to love coordinating weddings in village halls. The couples had to be inventive with their decorations and themes for the day and each one would look very different. If you like dancing, a village hall is perfect for a Ceilidh! You will usually need to clear up after one of these weddings on the night but depends on if the hall is being used the following day or not.

Barns

Barns are very popular in the UK and, again, these do tend to suit the more rustic, country look, although since most of them are just a big space, you can go for any theme you like. These may or may not have a bar or kitchen attached. Some have more facilities than others, so don't assume they are all the same. You might be looking at hiring the same things as a marquee depending on what is available.

Things to look out for when choosing a venue and questions to ask

- What time can you stay until? Some venues have a license to a certain time only. This might not work if you are party animals and want to be partying all night.
- When can you get into the venue to decorate? A marquee or barn will usually be available a couple of days before. A hotel or hall might not be available until the morning of the wedding - will this be a problem? If you have a venue decorator or wedding coordinator, this will not be a problem as they can get the venue ready while you are getting ready.
- Does the venue allow a band? You will be surprised that some venues won't, usually because they are in a noise abatement area and it is difficult

to regulate the volume of a band.

- Can you bring your own alcohol? If the venue has its own bar then you will need to check whether you can bring your own drinks (i.e. for the table or toasts). Sometimes they will charge corkage on each bottle opened. If you hire a bar company (I will discuss that in a later chapter) to serve the drinks and it is a cash bar, they will often have a clause that guests cannot bring their own drinks. Often, an exception is made for the champagne for the toast drinks but do check with the venue and bar company.
- What time do you need to vacate the premises?
- Do you need to clean before you go? Most venues will expect a certain level of cleaning to be done.
- What is the deposit to cover damages?
- What is included in the hire? E.g. some venues include use of the kitchen or a fridge for an outside caterer and some don't.

What do you need to hire?

If you have chosen a venue where you need to hire everything, then you need to make sure you do have everything.

- Electricity source. Do you need a generator and who will be in charge of turning it on and off, or adding fuel? How many sockets will you need?
- Heating - essential to hire in a marquee (even in the UK summer).
- Lighting
- Flooring - different types available for marquees. You might want to hire a dance floor even in a venue with a floor (e.g. barns or village halls).

These will be required for a marquee as the flooring is usually carpet or matting and not good for dancing on.

- Tables can seat 8-10 people depending on the size chosen (five or six-foot rounds, for example). So, how many guests do you want at each table? If you have eighty guests and sit eight to a table, you will need ten tables. If you seat ten, you will need eight larger tables. What about the top table? How many will sit on that? Do you want a traditional long table or a round one?
- You will also need extra tables for the cake, the gift table, welcome table (if required), if doing your own bar, you need one for the drinks, what about a buffet? You will need tables for that if the caterer is not bringing them. Does the DJ need a table? It's best to get a couple more than you think you need.
- Same for the chairs. Get a few extra. Five or six more than the total number is usually enough. Suppliers might need chairs during the day - e.g. musicians.
- Don't forget to include yourselves in the numbers!

I coordinated the wedding day of a couple in a marquee and I got there to find no chairs on the top table. I used the seating plan I had been given to make sure the right number of chairs were at each table as they all had ten chairs, even though some tables were seating eight or nine guests. However, I discovered they were still a few chairs short. I think they had forgotten to include themselves in the numbers when hiring the chairs. So, always hire a few more than you think you need.

- Don't forget tablecloths. You will need them for the main tables but also to cover the additional tables as well. Tablecloths come in different sizes. Do you want them to reach the floor? The hire company will be able to advise on sizes based on the table size.

I got to one venue where I was told everything would be set up and ready for me only to find some tables didn't have tablecloths. I think the couple had missed off the top table which usually needs three tablecloths to cover it. I had to send someone to the nearest supermarket to buy some large white paper tablecloths at short notice and we dressed the tables the best we could. Once the florist had finished and the table runners were on with the floral arrangements and all the glassware had been added, it didn't look too noticeable that some tables did not have fabric tablecloths. I started carrying emergency tablecloths in my wedding planning kit after that!

- Bar hire - are you getting a company in to run the bar?
- Glassware - do you need to hire this? Is the bar providing this for the tables as well as the bar? Are the caterers providing these?
- Catering Equipment - I will cover this in the next chapter.

Summary

- View your chosen venues
- Pick a venue and date (linked to the ceremony chapter)
- Make a list of what you need to hire

Wedding Notes

CHAPTER 4
CATERING

"If you live to be a hundred, I want to live to be a hundred minus one day, so I never have to live without you." — A. A. Milne

Catering can make or break a wedding. You do not want the one thing people remember about the day to be awful food or poor service from the catering staff. You also want to reflect your own personality in the food choice as you did for the venue. If you are a chilled-out couple who like to go with the flow and are planning an informal wedding in a field, choosing a four-course sit-down silver service wedding breakfast would be out of character. Likewise, if you have spent a small fortune hiring a castle for the weekend and hate eating with your fingers, then a barbeque buffet just won't do. Cater to the style of wedding you have. So, what are the main options?

Catering Options

Plated Meal

This is a three or four-course meal served to you at your table by waiters and waitresses. It usually involves a starter, main meal, and dessert followed by tea/coffee. Perfect for the traditional wedding. Pros: Everyone knows what to expect. Food is brought to everyone and plates are cleared quickly. Cons: Expensive and need plenty of staff, food wastage if guests don't eat, takes time to serve everyone and clear up, need a venue with good kitchen facilities or a caterer that has the equipment to cater for this in a venue without a kitchen.

Buffet

This can cover a whole range of food ideas and is usually reserved for a more casual wedding. A cold buffet is the budget option (think sandwiches, quiche, salads, pasta and rice salads, cheese and crackers, cold meats, etc.). Then you can have a hot buffet, where there is a choice of hot dishes. Asian cuisine works well here as do hotpots or casseroles. The advantage of this style is that it is usually less expensive than plated meals, waste is minimised and the guests can choose what they want. You will need to opt for easy to serve options as there will be a line of hungry guests waiting. Another option is to have a served buffet, where two or three staff serve the hot food which can keep the lines moving quickly. The Pros: Less expensive than a plated meal, plenty of variety and choice. Cons: You and your guests have to queue up (unless someone gets your meal for you), and popular dishes might have run out before all the guests get there.

Family Style

I love this one. It gives your reception a homely feel and gets guests interacting. Shareable dishes are placed on each table on sharing platters and everyone on the table dishes it out between them. This saves people lining up at buffet stations and no one risks missing out on food options because they were last in line.
That happened at a wedding I was a guest at once - our table was called last and there were slim pickings!
Pros: This works well for many varieties of cuisine, no one misses out on the options, and it gets guests interacting more. Cons: Need plenty of table space, so you would need to plan table decorations accordingly. If you were planning on covering the centre of your long tables with pretty vases and candles, you might have to rethink (I will discuss this more in Chapter 6).

Cocktail Style

You could skip the banquet style and seating plan completely and go with serving canapes and the guests stand to eat. The pros: Often the least expensive option, can go creative with the menu. Cons: You are likely to drop Satay sauce on your outfit, your Grandma will want to sit down, you will all be hungry a couple of hours later and if you do not get the food to alcohol ratio right, you may all be very drunk.

Barbeques and Hog Roasts

This is a great summer option, especially if your venue does not have a kitchen (think barns and marquees). Very popular in the UK and often combines with a buffet to complement the barbeque or hog roast. The hog roast is usually set up early in the morning and cooks all day. Pros: Everyone loves a barbeque! Informal, easy to manage in a field. Cons: That is unless your guests are vegetarian and vegan! Although there are some great options for veggies and vegans these days, so they won't be left out. Not so good if it rains and everyone must head out in the rain to get their food (need large umbrellas on hand).

Street Food Vendors

A popular trend, in the UK at least, is hiring street food vendors who park their vans outside the venue and the guests go and choose what they want from the vendor (obviously the guests don't get their wallets out - it's prepaid). Popular ones include fish and chips and Indian food. This can be a very economical catering choice, especially if somewhere with little amenity access. Pros: The vendors are used to mass catering from their van so will bring everything they need. You can also hire coffee vans, so you don't need to supply everything to make tea and coffee. Cons: Again, if it rains, the guests need to go out in the rain to get their food.

Why's it called a wedding breakfast? I hear you ask. Well, it's because it is the first meal after your wedding.

Evening Catering

Depending on the timing of the wedding breakfast and how many additional guests are coming, the following options are popular. A simplified buffet, breads and cheeses, pâté, etc. or hot sandwiches - e.g. bacon sandwiches (or the veggie equivalent), chips and pizza go down well. You could also hire your street vendors to do kebabs late into the night if you so wish.

What is the caterer responsible for?

The caterers should create the menu with your input and would normally be responsible for providing:

- All the food (including canapés)
- Waiting staff
- Drinks on the tables (most large catering companies provide a wine list and will also provide glassware for the tables, though this could be covered by the bar)
- Bar staff (if required, if a bar company is hired then they will provide this)
- Linen, cutlery and crockery (some couples hire the linen separately, especially if they want colourful tablecloths or other non-standard linen)
- Equipment for catering area (if required)

How can you help your caterer? And wedding day situations to avoid!

Working with your caterer - it's not all menu tasting and roses. What do they need to know from you to make it easier and smoother?

Are you planning speeches between courses? Make sure the caterer knows so they can plan!

I once coordinated a wedding in a marquee where the Father of the Bride gave a forty-five-minute speech in the space between the starter and the main course. The caterer was expecting fifteen minutes at the most and they had chicken keeping warm ready to serve! So, I had to deal with a caterer asking me to unplug the microphone on the man who probably paid for most of it! It was getting tense in the tent! Luckily, the food survived, although a bit dry.

So, be aware, if you get the timing wrong or disappear to take photos for hours, then the caterers will get upset and the food could be ruined.

The caterer will likely need running water and electricity. So, make sure this is available and accessible at the point they will need it. Most caterers will view the location of the wedding beforehand so should already know what they need and what is available. Make sure there is a hose pipe available if needed and plenty of sockets in the catering tent.

Do you need to hire equipment for the caterer to use? If they are setting up in a marquee kitchen tent, do you need to provide heaters, portable ovens, stainless steel worktops, etc.? The caterer should know what they need and either be able to hire it themselves or already have it. Don't assume though!

How many people are you actually catering for? Make sure the caterer knows this number.

I once coordinated the day of a marquee wedding for eighty-five guests where the couple had hired a caterer to cater for sixty people and then they were supplying additional food from another source. The official caterer was not happy with this as their insurance wouldn't cover the additional food, and if people got ill, would they know which food caused it? That's not the point I'm making here, but something to be aware of. So, when the caterers arrived to set the tables, they had only brought enough crockery and cutlery for sixty people, not eighty-five as they were not given this number. Luckily, we were on the site of a pub and they kindly lent us plates and cutlery. So, always make sure the person supplying the tableware knows the numbers! Incidentally, this was also the wedding where over ninety guests turned up and there wasn't enough seating so we had to drag in a table from the beer garden! - Always thinking on my feet.

This is where the seating plan helps, so you can make sure you hire the right number of tableware, chairs and tables. In this case, I don't think the couple had kept a record of who had replied - or maybe some guests forgot to RSVP!

Sometimes this can also go awry if you are supplying all the crockery and cutlery yourselves.

I supplied a DIY bride with a full list of items and quantities she needed to cater for the wedding party of 200 guests. So, how they ended up on the day with only 60 sets of cutlery and a bag of plastic spoons I'll never know. Trying to eat a Caribbean hot buffet with a plastic spoon is not easy.

If you are giving your guests a choice of food that they choose in advance, DO keep a record of this. Not just fifty people want the beef and forty want the chicken. The caterer needs to know who ordered what and where they are sitting so they send the correct dishes to the tables. If the guests can't remember what they chose or change their minds on the day, there will be a lot of disgruntled guests towards the end of the serving who have to have what dishes are left and not what they ordered. You also get an unhappy caterer as they have to field the complaints. So, make sure you have an Excel sheet with these details on and, better still, add the food choice to the back of the place names so the guests also know what they ordered. The caterer will also need to know where anyone with special dietary requirements is sitting. Most caterers can cater for people with allergies and intolerances as long as they know in advance. Telling them on the day that someone is Coeliac when every dish includes flour will not be helpful to them or your poor guest.

A list of useful questions to ask your caterer can be found at the back of the book.

Do you cater for your suppliers on the day?

This is something most people planning a wedding forget about or worry that they don't know if they should. Some suppliers may have a clause in their contract, so that is a good place to look.

Suppliers who are with you all day, e.g. photographer or wedding planner, would expect to be fed but will not expect to be seated with the guests. This is a break for them and so they will be happy to hide away to eat and take a breather for 30 minutes.

I was once put on the seating plan and had a place at one of the tables, but as I was still working, I had to keep getting up to deal with things. I would have been happier in the kitchen.

You do not need to cater with the same food as the guests if the budget does not allow for the extra mouths (and at some venues, you could be looking at £45-60 per person!), but some food would be appreciated. Evening suppliers - e.g. the band or DJ, would expect to join in with the evening buffet during the breaks and might have this in their contract.

It is also good form to have soft drinks or tea and coffee included. Alcoholic drinks would be at your discretion. As a wedding planner, it is nice to toast the happy couple with a bit of bubbly, but we are working.
If you are unsure, just ask them!

Summary

- Contact two or three caterers for menu ideas and prices and to check availability
- Meet the caterer at your chosen venue to check if what you require is feasible
- Discuss your budget (cost per person)
- Work with your caterer to create a menu based on the different catering options
- Have a tasting nearer the wedding day to finalise your options
- Decide who's providing the table drinks and glassware
- Decide if you are catering for suppliers on the day and what you will provide

Wedding Notes

CHAPTER 5
BAR HIRE AND DRINKS

"When you realize you want to spend the rest of your life with somebody, you want the rest of your life to start as soon as possible." — When Harry Met Sally

If you are getting married in a venue with a bar included, such as a hotel or country house, then the venue will provide the drinks and you will liaise with the venue coordinator to choose your drinks package. Guests would expect, at a minimum, a welcome drink, wine on the tables and a drink for the toast. A typical drinks package might include 2 glasses of wine per person, or half a bottle. Or you could order a set number of bottles per table. Then the venue's fully stocked bar will provide all other drinks.

The Welcome Drink

This is often champagne, prosecco, bucks fizz or Pimms, but you could offer a signature cocktail instead. At least one drink per person. A bottle of fizz usually does 8 glasses, so you will need 13 bottles for 100 guests. If you are offering more than one drink, then you will need to double the number of bottles. Don't forget to offer soft drinks as well for non-drinkers and children. Especially if it is a hot day, you may be surprised how many guests will go for the non-alcoholic option.

Reception Drinks

It is normal to provide wine on the tables. How many you put is up to you. If you know from your seating plan one table has lots of children on it, you will need fewer bottles than a table of all adults. If you go with half a bottle per person, then a table of 8 adults could get through 4 bottles of wine over a 3-hour meal. You will also need to provide a jug of water. If you know there are plenty of non-drinkers, providing a good quality non-alcoholic wine is essential. There are some very good ones around so do some testing.

The Toast

As with the welcome drink, the rule is one glass per guest. With eight glasses per bottle, you will need 13 bottles for 100 hundred guests. Obviously, children won't be partaking and some guests will say no, but as a rule, this will be enough. If you are not in a hotel, you will need to arrange for someone, quite often the caterer, to pour these drinks before the speeches.

I have coordinated a couple of weddings where they did a cork popping. So, the champagne was on the tables and then one person on each table had to pop the corks at the same time when given the instruction to do so. Then that person either poured the toast drinks for everyone or the bottle was passed around the table. This is a lovely way to get guests involved.

Personalised Cocktails

These are popular for the modern wedding. Couples are choosing a few select cocktails to serve at their wedding receptions. These could be themed around your wedding theme (having a glitzy, James Bond wedding? Got to be the vodka martini, shaken not stirred, or for a rustic wedding, how about the old-fashioned?). If you're a fan of gin, you can hire gin bars and offer different gins and tonics with garnishes.

Bar Options

So, once you have supplied the welcome drink, table wine and toast drink, what are the options for the bar?

Supplying your own

Lee, from Louisianna's Mobile Bars, offers this advice on supplying your own drinks for the day: If you are supplying all your own alcohol for a bar, you need to be clear about how much you are going to need. The two worst things that can happen are: you won't have enough and run out halfway through the evening, or you will buy far too much, which is a waste of money. Make sure you get plenty, but get it on sale or return, so unused bottles can be returned for a refund.

If you are supplying your own alcohol. You will need:
- A bar
- Fridges
- Ice
- Straws
- Fruit
- Glassware (lots of it!)
- Corkscrews and bottle openers
- Bins
- Bin bags
- Recycling of bottles
- Staff

Staff is very important if you don't want it turning into a free for all. Guests might take more than they should (a 25ml measure of a spirit becomes half a tumbler), or open bottles and leave them to go to waste. If a guest gets too intoxicated, bar staff will be experienced with dealing with them and will be able to limit the amount of alcohol they consume. Staff will also help clear away at the end of the night and have everything organised for you.

Another added advantage of staff is that it is a better experience for the guests to have their drinks prepared and served and they are less likely to abuse the generosity of the couple who is supplying the drinks. Also, it could get very messy with drinks being spilt, bottles lying around or someone disappearing with the bottle opener. Staff will have control and will keep the drinks area clean and tidy.

How much do you need for a full bar?

There is a wide variety to choose from, and do you choose the basics or a wider selection?

- Wine - red, white and a rose.
- Sparkling wine or Prosecco and/or champagne.
- Beer - draft or bottles/cans. Just one sort or a mix of larger, bitter or stout.
- Spirits - Gin, Vodka, Whisky, Rum, Brandy, other types.
- Soft drinks - water, cordial, lemonade, cola, fruit juices etc.
- Mixers - tonic, ginger ale, soda water, bitter lemon.

Bridebox.com offers advice on how much to supply for stocking the bar for a wedding party of 100 guests (this does not include reception drinks):

- Beer - 7 cases of beer (24 bottles per case = 168 bottles) as not everyone will drink beer.
- Bottles of wine = 24 bottles = 120 glasses of wine.
- Spirits are trickier as you won't know what the guests will drink. If in doubt, go for 4 bottles of vodka, 2 bottles of gin, 2 bottles of rum and 2 bottles of whisky.
- 33 bottles of assorted mixers

- 100 pounds of ice
- Garnishes - mint, lemon, lime etc.

http://www.bridebox.com/blog/alcohol-at-wedding/

Hiring a mobile bar company

This is the easiest and, actually, the more cost-effective option, as Lee explains:
If you are buying all your own drinks, you need to think about hiring, cleaning, returning glassware. You need to shop for and store the alcohol before the wedding day. You need to hire fridges. You need to know who is chilling it and how it will be served. If you hire a mobile bar, like Louisianna's, they will be able to do this for you, whether that is with your own table wine and toast drinks, or by providing everything. A professional bar company means you have less to think about and you will have a fully stocked bar to cater for all your guests' tastes, staff to serve all the drinks and clean used glasses, and they will clean up at the end of the night. They will also provide the licence to sell alcohol. One thing this means is that if you hire a bar, then your guests will not be permitted to bring their own alcohol to the wedding.

Mobile bars, in general, will very often provide a free set-up in return for a minimum spend by the guests. This means you don't have to worry about anything to do with the drinks on the day and if the guests are paying anyway, you are not spending money on the drinks other than the main ones listed earlier. So, if you're having a budget wedding, hiring a mobile bar to provide the drinks to paying guests is more cost-effective than buying them yourself.

One thing that is important to note, if you are hiring a cash bar but you or your caterer are supplying the day drinks, is who is supplying all the glassware? It would make sense for the bar to provide all the glassware used throughout the day, otherwise, it all gets mixed up. I have coordinated many a wedding day where the caterer was supplying glasses for the table and then guests were buying drinks from the bar with the bar glasses and it can then be difficult to make sure all the glassware is going back to the correct supplier!

Summary

- Decide if you are providing the drinks yourself or using a supplier
- Is the caterer or the bar company providing the reception/table/toast drinks?
- If providing your own: How much do you need to buy?
- What drinks do you want to serve for the drinks reception and toast?
- How will you chill the drinks?
- Who will serve the drinks?
- Do you need to hire glassware and jugs?
- Who will clear and wash the glasses?
- What to expect from a mobile bar hire company.

Wedding Notes

CHAPTER 6
DECORATIONS AND FLOWERS

"Marriages, like a garden, take time to grow. But the harvest is rich unto those who patiently and tenderly care for the ground." — Darlene Schacht

So, you have found your perfect venue and now you need to decorate it. If you have chosen a venue like a castle or stately home that is already beautiful, you will probably want to keep to a more traditional look with lots of flowers in colours that suit your theme and the venue.

If you have a blank canvas venue, like a marquee or village hall, then you will need to be more imaginative to make the venue look fabulous.

What are the options?

Marquee liners, starlight backdrops and other fabric drapes are great for transforming places that need a lot of covering. You can hire marquee liners and convert the inside of a village hall or function room to look like the inside of a marquee.

I did a wedding where the couple had chosen a sports hall for the venue. Think more badminton court than reception venue. A company installed marquee linings and carpets and it looked and felt like a marquee once it was dressed and not a giant echoey sports hall.

Putting a starlight backdrop at one end of a hall or the marquee can give focus to the top table or the band in the evening and can cover a multitude of sins, such as the old function room's dodgy décor or weird art.

Table Decor

Flowers

Flowers are not the only option! But I will discuss them first.

Floral arrangements are the mainstay of a wedding. You can have low arrangements, tall vases, candelabras, or lots of little vases. The bigger the arrangement, the more expensive it is. Flowers are not cheap - unless you have grown them yourself from seed ready to use for the wedding. If you are budget conscious, choose flowers that are in season. The more exotic or difficult to get, the more expensive. You can always add more greenery to bulk out your arrangements. If you tell your florist your budget per table, they can give you options.

You will need to factor in the cost of hiring vases or candelabras if using these. If you hire these from a florist, you won't be able to take your arrangements home or give them as gifts. If you want to do this, have arrangements where you have purchased the whole thing and not hired any elements.

When it comes to thinking about the type of arrangements you want, think about your tables, the size and shape. If you want guests to chat across the table, go for low arrangements or tall thin arrangements with the flowers up high. You don't want all the arrangements blocking the view the guests have of each other or the top table.

If you are planning on family-style platters on the table for the meal, then you need arrangements that won't get in the way. All those platters and plates take up a lot of space and if you crowd the table with hundreds of little jars of flowers and candles, the caterer will struggle to serve the food and your arrangements will get messed up or removed from the tables.

If you got married at a church or registry office and you had a floral arrangement for the ceremony, this can be used on your top table.
Where else can flowers be used? Cake table, or decorating the cake, pedestals at the entrance to the room or marquee, and hanging from a cartwheel over the dance floor - this looks great in those Tee-pee or Yurt tents.

What table centre alternatives are there?

Balloons are popular - and as they float, you can keep them up high so no one has an obscured view. They also make quite an impact and are cost-effective options that come in many colours.

Books - I coordinated one wedding where the couple had created the table centres with books.

If the venue allows, you can have candles or lanterns on the table. Or use LED candles if real flames are not allowed. Or how about glass jars filled with battery fairy lights?

Photo by Joe Stenson

What else goes on the tables?

Menu, place cards, table numbers or names, you can add cameras and little trivia games. Wedding favours are often added for the guests, which are little gifts for each guest. Activity books for children. Tables can get quite crowded once the crockery, cutlery, glassware, water jugs, wine bottles and napkins get added!

Lighting

Coloured lights in the corners of the marquee or hall add interest and are an easy way to add atmosphere. They look great lighting up a white marquee when viewed from the outside. Strings of fairy lights everywhere are pretty and a cost-effective lighting option. Battery versions are very useful to put in areas where there are no plug sockets available

Most marquee companies provide lighting as part of their packages. Make sure you have lighting outside the marquee as well. Guests like to sit outside on an evening and will also need lighting to find the toilets in the dark. Solar lighting would work well outside and is easy to install.

Foliage and Lanterns

Foliage and pot plants can be hired. I did one wedding where the couple hired large pots of bamboo to line the entrance to the venue. Another couple had a Moroccan style tent and used large plants and pots to decorate. Large lanterns can be used inside and outside.

Chair Covers and Table Runners

Chair covers are only really essential if the chairs are hideous and don't go with your wedding look or are the wrong colour for your theme. There are various options available and different sizes, so you might need to check your chair sizes. Table runners are a personal choice. But if you use them, you will need to make sure they all run in the same direction (it's the attention to detail that's important).

Bouquets and Floral Accessories

Bouquets

There many choices when it comes to bouquets. Do you prefer fresh or silk flowers? Do you want to carry something that isn't flowers, such as a brooch or button bouquet, a feather fan or fabric flower pomander?

If you choose a fresh flower bouquet, what style do you like? There are many options available such as round, hand-tied, cascade, crescent, posy, nosegay, pageant - to name just a few.

The bouquet you choose needs to compliment your wedding style and bridal gown. A cascade bouquet or a formal round bouquet is perfect for a traditional wedding with a princess style or A-line wedding dress. If you're having a more relaxed boho wedding, then a simple hand-tied posy would suit. Pageant style bouquets that sit into and over the crook of the arm look great with more form-fitting dresses like sheath or mermaid style.

Bridesmaids will often have a smaller, simpler version of the bridal

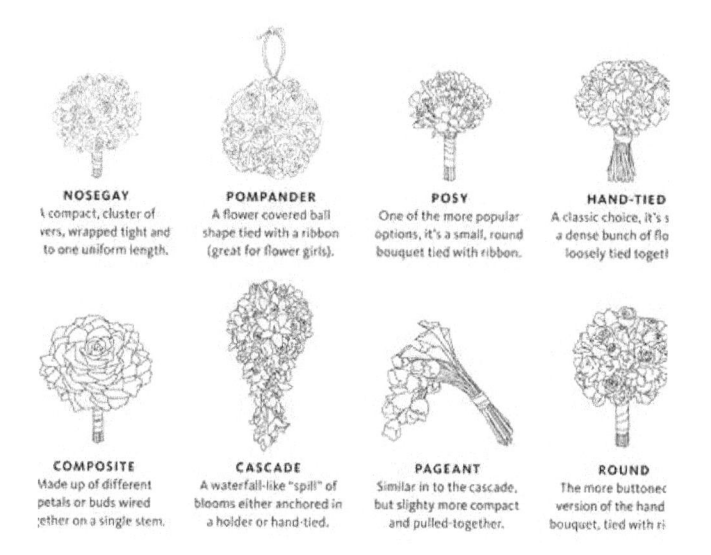

NOSEGAY	POMPANDER	POSY	HAND-TIED
A compact, cluster of vers, wrapped tight and to one uniform length.	A flower covered ball shape tied with a ribbon (great for flower girls).	One of the more popular options, it's a small, round bouquet tied with ribbon.	A classic choice, it's s a dense bunch of flo loosely tied toget!

COMPOSITE	CASCADE	PAGEANT	ROUND
Made up of different petals or buds wired ;ether on a single stem.	A waterfall-like "spill" of blooms either anchored in a holder or hand-tied.	Similar in to the cascade, but slighty more compact and pulled-together.	The more buttoned version of the hand bouquet, tied with ri

This photo (taken from www.theknot.com) shows the main different styles.

bouquet, but this can depend on how many bridesmaids you have and your budget.

On the day, make sure the stems have been dried before putting the bouquet near your dress.

Buttonholes and Corsages

These are for men and women and it is usually safest to wear them all upright and on the left so that it looks symmetrical in the photos when everyone is all lined up. There is a superstition about this that I mention in Chapter 15.

Advice from a Floral Consultant:

Kath Lambert, a floral consultant in Leeds, gives the following advice for getting the best out of your floral designer, florist or venue stylist:

- When requesting quotes, it is helpful to have photos of the styles you like. Most florists will be able to gauge the cost of a bouquet or arrangement from looking at a photo.
- The increased use of social media is causing a lack of interaction between the florist and client. It is really important to have a personal connection with your suppliers so that you both have an understanding of what is required.
- Most florists will want to meet you so they can make sure you get what you are wanting, their reputation is on the line.
- It's acceptable to make contact via social media, but follow up with a phone call and/or a face-to-face meeting.
- Go to wedding fairs and open days/evenings at your chosen venue to meet florists and venue stylists who have worked there. This is a good time to meet them in person, especially if you don't live in the area you are getting married.
- It's ok to meet your florist without knowing what you want. A good florist will be able to make suggestions based on the venue, budget and colour scheme and will give you advice to guide you to what you do want.
- Visit florists close to your home and near the wedding venue. If you are having a large wedding, florists and stylists who specialise in them will be prepared to travel.
- A prospective client should be able to see the florist or venue stylist's

previous work and get testimonials from former clients.

- Florists can work with other established suppliers to get everything you need for the floral arrangements and styling the venue. By using one point of contact, working with just the one company should save you time, stress and money, as opposed to having to source all the elements yourself from different suppliers (e.g. chair covers from one supplier, table centres from another, bouquets from another, lighting and drapes from yet another supplier, etc.).

What is the timeline for choosing your florist and styles of flowers?

Visit your floral choices as soon as you have booked your venue. Like all suppliers, the best ones get booked up early. Have a few to visit and go for consultations. The best way to find out what you want is to chat it through with them. Once you have decided, book them and pay your deposit. You will work out the details later.

Meet up with them once you have the dresses sorted and bring swatches of fabrics with you. This is usually about 6 months before. You will go through the budget, style and options at this meeting. This will be when a formal quotation can be given. Most florists do not tie you into anything at this stage as there is still time to change what you want.

A month to six weeks before the wedding day, you will need final numbers (e.g. for chair covers, tables centres, number of buttonholes, bouquets, etc.)

and to finalise the details. The florist can then create your invoice which is usually due two weeks before the day.

Kath offers a couple of other pieces of advice:
Do your research. Beware of Facebook suppliers who can pop up with pretty photos and great testimonials, and then disappear again. Venue decorators can come and go. Make sure you check them out on online forums - see what other people are saying and what the feedback is like. There's nothing wrong with choosing a venue stylist off Facebook, but do more than just a quick Google search before handing over your money. And never pay the full amount upfront, just pay the deposit and wait to pay the remainder nearer to the wedding day. You never know what can happen in the space of a year and you run the risk of losing more than the deposit if they stop trading before your wedding day. This advice covers all suppliers and not just florists or venue stylists.

CHAPTER 7
PHOTOGRAPHY

"For it was not into my ear you whispered, but into my heart. It was not my lips you kissed, but my soul."
— Judy Garland

This is quite often a large expense on the wedding day and for a decent photographer, you will be looking at £750 upwards. According to Hitched.co.uk, the average spend on a photographer in 2019 was £1155. It is possible to spend less on a photographer, but they might not be experienced and might not have all the backup equipment required to avoid any wedding day issues. A way of saving some money could be to book them just to cover the ceremony and group shots. Remember that a good chunk of the work for the photographer is after the wedding day when they have to process and edit the photos. Some photographers take longer than others for this stage. Check the contract to find out how soon you can have access to your photos.

When I got married, our photographer just covered the ceremony, group shots, a few posed photos, pretending to cut the cake, and then he took some reportage style photos during the drinks reception and was gone before the wedding breakfast. After the wedding, he, unfortunately, had family issues and we had to wait ages for him to process the photo choices we made. This was pre-digital and we could choose 30 photos from a selection of about 75 only! In the end, he gave us a copy of all of them! So, problems can happen and at least we still got photos.

It is absolutely fine to hire a wedding photographer at the start of their career, just as long as you know that is the case. Everyone needs to start somewhere.

Different types of photographers

Traditional

Traditional photographers are great at the formal wedding shots and will spend hours setting up group shots and posed photos. They like to capture the perfect moments of the wedding day. You will get excellent, but sometimes formulaic photos. You might need one of the wedding party to be a runner to collect guests for particular shots. You also need to be aware of the timing. A photographer who takes hundreds of different posed shots often forgets there is a wedding breakfast waiting.

Photojournalism or Reportage

You will probably have seen this term used on photographer websites and in bridal magazines. This is where the photographer documents the day without any staged shots, although they will usually still take the group shots you need. You will get 'candid' shots of the guests chatting, the looks between the couples, kids being cute, that sort of thing. You will see lots of things that happened at the wedding that you won't have noticed on the day. They specialize in the close-up reactions to the events.

Commercial Photographer

These will be great at capturing the décor, flowers, cake, centrepieces, etc. They might not be 'people' photographers, but you will get high-quality images.

Photographic Artist

This photographer rarely takes traditional shots but will find artistic ways to photograph the different elements. They often work in black and white, full of drama and artistry. I worked with a photographer like this on a few of my weddings and loved watching her work and create these amazing photos.

I think the best photography is a mix of traditional and reportage. Get your formal shots done quickly and then get on with your day while the photographer documents what's going on. They will also get all the detail shots of the tables and cake. Be aware that if the photographer gets to the venue after guests have sat down or dumped their bags and coats at the tables, then they won't get photos of the tables undisturbed. Maybe make sure one of your guests who's handy with a camera can take some when they get there to make sure these shots are not missed. As a wedding coordinator, I always took photos of the venues when they were finished being dressed. The venue dresser will also do the same, so you can always ask them if they took photos you could use. These will not be professional standard though.

Advice from a photographer

Paula Brown, the photographer at Ollivision, offers words of advice on her blog (www.ollivision.co.uk).

The photographer needs to have two cameras, as even an experienced photographer can have a camera stop working on them, and if that's during a part of the day that can't be repeated (e.g. the ceremony), you want to know they can just pick up their other camera and continue shooting. Likewise, an additional flash is a must. If it is an evening event, the flash is crucial and if that stops working, you will have no usable photos.

When choosing a photographer, what should you look out for?

- Ask to see three full weddings that they have photographed, ask for the client logins for the client photo galleries. If they are unable to do that, it might mean they have not done any weddings yet.
- Check the quality of the photos they do show you – are there harsh flash shadows, burnt-out white areas with details missing, grainy appearance - often from over-correction of an exposure error, couples appearing dark when backlit by lights or windows, red dots on dark areas of the photos – these are all things a decent photographer can avoid with the photography and the processing afterwards.
- Check they have a contract and they ask for a deposit. This works both ways and the contract is the written agreement that they are obliged to shoot your wedding and you are obliged to pay them.

Paula has had last-minute calls from brides where the photographer has let them down a week before or even on the wedding day itself! All the couples had the same thing in common – no contract and no deposit paid.

- A professional photographer will have professional indemnity and public liability insurance.
- A professional photographer makes their living from photography and therefore charges professional rates.

I always made sure I had a good relationship with the photographers I worked with and they would be great at calling me from the ceremony venue to let me know the guests were on their way and we should get the reception drinks ready.

Summary

- Choose the style of photography you prefer
- Choose your photographer with care
- Meet with a few you like or have recommended
- Book your photographer

Wedding Notes

CHAPTER 8
VIDEOGRAPHY

"You don't marry the person you can live with—you marry the person you can't live without."
— Unknown

Some photographers can offer a fixed, unmanned camera that can do video, so this can be set up to film the ceremony or the speeches. A videography company will be able to film with roaming cameras, multiple cameras and even with drones! Obviously, costs vary depending on the amount of coverage and editing required. A lot of the time and expense is in the editing. A full wedding can be edited down to 15-30 minutes. Just check with the company what you get. Often, they will do a short five-minute highlights version, and then a longer version plus ceremony.

Becki and James from 2 Little Ducks Wedding Videography (love that name!) give advice on choosing a videographer:

- What do you want the film to do? Is it an emotional quick reminder of the day or a verbatim account? Some videographers will offer a five-minute "highlight" of the day only while others offer service and speeches in full with other parts of your day done in a montage.
- There are not many videographers around now that will just press record for the whole day and hand over the footage.
- The art of good videography is all in the editing, so do make sure

you see lots of examples. If you are looking for a full, documentary-style hour-long film, this is unlikely to be on the business website so you may have to ask to have one sent to you in order to see how your final film will look.

- What style of film do you want? The options are cinematic and documentary, although most videographers do mix a bit of both.
- Do you want them to film from afar and not get in the way or do you want to set up shots and spend lots of time on this? This will eat into your time with your guests and you have to factor in photoshoots as well. A lot of videographers will tag along with the photographer to get the couple shots, however, movement works better for the film rather than posed shots.
- What is your budget? The more videographers filming on the day, the more footage and interesting shots, multiple angles you will get, but the more it will cost. Single shooters are less intrusive and usually cheaper but may struggle with the variety of equipment that is needed to set up to ensure good coverage throughout the day.

How can you support your videographer to get the best results?

- To support your videographer, you will need to make them aware of as much about the running order of your day as you possibly can.

Becki and James were filming a wedding at Rudding Park - "There is a deconsecrated church on-site and the couple told us that was where they were having their service. On the day, I filmed bridal prep and James set up the cameras and audio in the church. I just happened to pop down from bridal prep to see how James was getting on and overheard a hotel staff member directing some wedding guests away from the church and into a function room, I asked why he had done that when the service was in the church and was told that the blessing was in the church but the legal ceremony was in a function room in the hotel, in less than 15 minutes time!! I ran into the church grabbing at equipment and shouting to James. We managed to set up enough kit in the room to grab the ceremony but were sweating and panicking throughout, and then, of course, straight after the ceremony we had to move everything back into the church to film the blessing!! Four years on, I still cannot believe that the couple failed to tell us they were having two ceremonies!!"

- Do keep them informed on the day of any changes, letting your guests know if you want them to do guest messages, letting your bridal party know that there will be a videographer, so that if they are aware of any surprises, they can get in touch and prepare them, and being clear about any must-have shots or must have people in your film.

Surprises have got us a few times too, usually special heartfelt presents, singing waiters, surprise guests that have flown in! As we ask the couple, it is often someone else in the bridal party that has arranged something and not thought to let us (or the photographer) know. Once, a groom had arranged for his fiancée's primary school class to be in the church singing a song for them during the service. The bride was absolutely overwhelmed, everyone was in tears and though we filmed it, we didn't realise the significance until after.

What else do you need to know about videography?

- Make sure your photographer, if you are having one, either already has a good relationship with your videographer or at least that your photographer is OK about there being a videographer and aware that the video is just as important as the photos. The videographer often needs the same position as the photographer but it is much harder for them to move (audio and tripods) than the photographer. A lot of photographers can feel that they are more important, and on the day, this can lead to friction.
- Check with your venue (especially churches) that they allow videography.
- Check that the videographer has appropriate public liability insurance and especially a CAA permission to fly licence and specialist drone insurance if this is offered, most don't and a lot of venues will check.
- Music licences can be tricky. They can be purchased from the PRS website for films that are reproduced on DVD/Blu-ray. If they are uploaded to YouTube, then YouTube sort out the royalties to the artist, and artists that don't have this arrangement (e.g. The Beatles and Bruno Mars) will block your film on YouTube, so if you wanted to share on social media afterwards, you might struggle.

For information: Some churches will ask for a "filming/videography licence". No such licence exists and what most mean is the PRS licence as the service and many hymns are copyrighted. The PRS licence is for transferring the final film onto disc though (a mechanical reproduction licence) and does not need to be purchased beforehand. If your officiant is insisting on it, this is what they are talking about.

- Check the delivery platform your film will arrive in. DVDs will generally be poor-quality as the films are squashed onto a too-small disc. Blu-rays are better but a lot of people do not have this player. USBs are best and a lot of companies will do a digital platform, which is great for ease of sharing.
- Regardless of the number of videographers you have, they should have lenses/cameras that film well in low/night time light for the evening reception and, at the very least, a backup camera in case the first one fails.

It is also worth understanding that the video editing process takes time, a LOT of time, and like most suppliers, videographers make hay whilst the sun shines. This means that they can be out filming two to four days a week in high season and will not have much opportunity to edit. Contracts should make clear expectations of the timescale, but do be prepared to wait for a good product. Asking for raw footage is generally a no-no, the product is the edited film, not the ingredients. It is a bit like paying for your wedding dress and then asking the designer for the material and pattern so you can make another!

Summary

- Decide what you want the videography to do
- View your short-listed videographer's work
- Meet with a few you like or have recommended
- Book your videographer

Wedding Notes

CHAPTER 9

THE WEDDING CAKE

"To me, you are perfect."
—Love Actually

It has always been a tradition that cake plays an important part in the wedding. Originally, guests would bring small cakes to place in front of the couples. The couple would kiss over the pile of cakes to guarantee future prosperity (hitched.co.uk).

One of the many perks of the job was getting to eat a bit (er, a lot) of wedding cake. Gone are the days of fruit cake, marzipan and royal icing. In are the days of different flavours, personalisation and lots of imagination. Cake flavours like chocolate, red velvet, lemon, and ginger have taken over from fruit cake or vanilla sponge. It's so hard to choose a flavour, so couples are having a different flavour in every tier. And it's not just about tiered cakes either. So, let's look at the options.

Options

The Tiered Cake

Keeping with a traditional look is the tiered cake. This style of cake originated at the wedding of Prince Leopold, Duke of Albany in 1882. How high can you go? If it's a royal wedding then you need tiers upon tiers practically touching the ceiling. For us common folk, three or four tiers is the popular choice. The venue space and style might also dictate the style of cake. If the venue has high ceilings in a grand room, a little two-tier cake will get lost. In a small venue, a towering five-tier extravaganza would dominate the space. It depends on what kind of statement you want to make and what the budget is.

As mentioned, the cake flavours are up to you and you don't need fruit cake unless you want it. Each tier of the cake is made up of four-six layers of cake with a filling that is then iced, then each tier is stacked on top of each other and then the whole cake is decorated. You can also have false tiers. So, if you want the look of a five-tier cake but only need four tiers, have a fake layer. This will be iced and decorated like the rest of the cake so won't really save you much money, but it will be unnoticeable to the guests. Just make sure the person cutting the cake knows which is the fake cake!

Round or Square? On a practical level, the square cake is easier to cut up into nice even slices. But square or round depends on what you prefer. You'll know which this is. Just make sure you hire the right shaped cake stand for the cake.

There are plenty of resources online to work out what size cake you need, and your cake maker will advise as well. But as a guide:
- Three round tiers of 6, 8 and 10 inches would give approximately 78 servings and four tiers of 6, 8, 10 and 12 inches would give approximately 134 servings.
- For square cakes, three tiers of 6, 8 and 10 inches is approximately 100 servings (22 more than round) and four tiers of 6, 8, 10 and 12 inches would give 172 servings (38 more than round).

Obviously, it depends on how big a slice you cut, smaller slices = more servings, bigger slices = fewer servings.

If budget is an issue, you can always have a smaller decorated cake and then a cutting cake, which is a plain iced cake that the guests don't see, that is cut up for extra portions.

At the end of the book, I include further information on cake portions and cutting the cake.

The Naked Cake

This is popular, especially for less formal weddings, and I've coordinated many weddings with naked cakes. If you don't know what this is, it's a tiered sponge cake (usually vanilla) with lots of thin layers and a jam and cream or buttercream filling with the layers and filling designed to be seen. There can be a thin layer of buttercream on the sides, but so the sponge still shows through, but no fondant or royal icing. This type of cake is decorated with a dusting of icing sugar, fresh fruit and/or flowers. If you hate all that sweet icing, then this is for you. These look lovely in a rustic setting, in a Tee-pee or barn wedding. The disadvantage is that without the protection of the icing, it can dry out, especially if in a warm marquee. These cakes need to be made the day before or the morning of the wedding. Also, the filling and fruit will attract insects if you are somewhere that's a bit more open to the elements. Wonky cake layers cannot be disguised by hiding under the icing.

The Novelty Cake

Semi-naked cake with thin layer of buttercream.

I love a novelty cake. You can really go to town with your theme, personalities, hobbies etc. with a novelty cake. These make a colourful focal point. Pinterest has so many photos of different ones to give you ideas.

I did one wedding where the cake was the groom's car with the groom's legs sticking out from underneath as if repairing it and the bride sat on the bonnet! Another looked like a traditional cake from one angle but had a rugby ball sticking out the side as if it had been kicked into the cake.

If you are going for the novelty cake, find a company that specialises in these cakes (otherwise, it will be funny for all the wrong reasons) and go to town with your ideas.

If you don't want a full novelty cake, you can go for a fun cake topper instead to sit on top or alongside a more traditional cake.

Cupcakes

This was a huge trend a while back. We had cupcakes at our wedding in 2003 and it was a novel idea back then! I do love the look of pretty cupcakes on a stand, and everyone gets their own individual cake. These can be made in different flavours as well and be decorated to fit your theme. This works for smaller weddings as you don't need too many cupcakes to make a great display - this isn't Cupcake Wars (anyone watch that? Or is it just me?). There is usually a high buttercream to cake ratio - so if you don't have a sweet tooth, it can be a bit too much.

Cake Selections

I have seen this at a couple of weddings where ten-fifteen guests (who can obviously bake) brought different cakes and they set up a cake buffet table. If you are doing this, make sure all cakes are labelled with any allergens and make sure there are cake options for people with intolerances (e.g. egg-free, nut-free, no dairy (vegan)). This gives lots of cake variety and is a cheap option as your guests are bringing them. They look great displayed on a long table and on different stands. But which one do you cut? And have they been labelled correctly?

The Brownie Tower

Who doesn't love a sticky chocolate brownie? I've seen these at a few weddings and they make a great display. The brownies are stacked to create a tower and, usually, fruit like raspberries are placed in between and around them. These are more difficult to build than you would think. This was evident when I was asked to create the brownie tower at one wedding (I had to Google it) and then watched from a distance during the speeches as the top few brownies fell off the display! There's obviously an art to it! I think I got it right on the next wedding that had them and I tried out my new skills. Live and learn. And eat brownies.

The Cake that Isn't a Cake

Cheese cakes are popular. Five round cheeses of decreasing size are stacked on top of each other like a cake and decorated with grapes. This is great as a display for the evening buffet and then can be eaten with crackers, chutneys and fruit. It can get a bit smelly if set up in a warm closed room for too long!

Cutting the cake

When is a good time to cut the cake? Traditionally, it was done after the speeches, while everyone was having their tea and coffee. A lot of couples are now choosing to wait until the evening to cut the cake. By doing this, the evening guests get to see the cake in all its glory. It works well with combining cutting the cake and then going straight into the first dance. The cake can then be served as part of the evening buffet. Moving the cake to be cut up is a two-person job! So, whoever is doing this needs help.

I often had the enviable job of cutting the wedding cake up to be served.

At one wedding, I coordinated in an amazing deconsecrated church, I went to do this and found that there were no platters to put the cake on. Luckily, we were not far from a supermarket and I was able to go and pick up some foil platters quite quickly and get back to the venue and finish cutting and serving the cake before anyone knew I had gone.

https://www.hitched.co.uk/wedding-planning/organising-and-planning/wedding-traditions-and-superstitions/

Wedding Notes

CHAPTER 10
ENTERTAINING YOUR GUESTS

"I hope you don't mind, I hope you don't mind that I put down in words. How wonderful life is, now you're in the world." — Elton John

Though you are undoubtedly the stars of the day, you also need to think about what to do to keep the guests entertained during the parts of the wedding where they are not watching you two do something. You can't have a wedding that is silent, and sometimes, there are stretches when not much seems to be happening and guests have a habit of wandering off. So, you will need some form of music or entertainment during the day. This chapter will go through the different parts of the wedding day and look at appropriate entertainment, it will also include all those extras that keep the guests occupied, such as candy carts, chocolate fountains and the photo booth.

Ceremony

During the ceremony, you will need music while guests arrive and are seated. You will need music for the entrance and exit and during the signing of the registrar. This can be a playlist, an organ, choir, string quartet, a friend with a guitar (are you picturing Four Weddings and a Funeral?) or something else that fits your wedding style.

Drinks Reception

During the drinks reception, you will want music playing. Again, this can just be a playlist or you can hire a jazz trio, string quartet, harpist, violinist, or singer, for example, to entertain during this part of the day. The musician you hired for the ceremony could continue during this part of the day.

Wedding Breakfast

During the meal, the guests are usually chattering away so you don't really need any musicians and can just use a playlist. However, I have been to weddings with entertainment during the meal. A magician works well, going to each table and doing close-up magic between courses. Or I did one with singing waiters. They start out looking like waiting staff and then usually create a bit of a comedic/awkward scene before launching into singing. It's funny watching the confusion before people realise it is an act.

The Evening

The evening entertainment should involve dancing and it is usually a choice between a DJ or a band. Bands can vary from a three-person band playing covers to a 12-piece blues band. The more band members – the more expensive they are. Ceilidhs are popular and are great for getting everyone up dancing.

This part of the day is perfect for the photo booth, chocolate fountain or candy carts. The candy carts are often set up quite early on, and if you have children at the wedding, stock may be limited come the evening! These can be hired in fully stocked, or you can create a sweets table yourself with lots of jars of sweets, those little plastic scoops and a pile of striped paper bags.

You can hire photo booths in all sorts of styles, from vintage to glamorous, to a car or campervan booth that can pull up to your venue and set up outside. You can also create your own photo booth by setting up a screened-off corner, providing a basket of props and a camera.

Fireworks are another favourite for later in the evening. Just check that your venue allows firework displays as not all of them do. It is best to get in professionals for this. A 6-minute display can cost around £600-£1200 depending on what you require.

Other Options

Other entertainment I've seen have included belly dancers, circus acts, bagpipers, drummers, caricature artists and bird of prey displays. So, if you can book it, you can have it.

When you book your entertainment, you need to know your venue and whether it is suitable for the entertainment you're booking. I already mentioned that not all venues allow bands. But what about access to your venue? Some venues are quite difficult to get to or the access is a long way from the function room. What if you need to get a harpist to the top floor of a hotel and the lift breaks down? Or the only access is up a large flight of steps? If you have an entertainer, like a belly dancer, who needs to get changed, have you got a room for them to change in?

I coordinated one wedding in a large hotel where the ceremony venue was on the ground floor and the drinks reception and wedding breakfast was two long corridors and a lift away. The couple wanted the musician from the ceremony, who was playing a large electric keyboard, to be playing for the drinks reception in the other room. With all the 250 guests filing out and up to the other room, and him having to unplug his equipment and find a trolley to transport it up the lift to the other floor, it was a good while before he could get set up again. I don't think the couple were very happy about this. So, be realistic with what is feasible for a normal human being!

Things to check with your entertainment:

- Do they have insurance? This is essential.
- What electrical requirements do they have?
- Do they need somewhere to get changed?
- Do they need access to the venue to set up early?
- What time will they arrive before they start?
- What parking do they need?

CHAPTER 11
TRANSPORT

"A marriage is always made up of two people who are prepared to swear that only the other one snores."
- Terry Pratchett

How you get about depends on where your wedding is and if you are changing venues. I got married and had the reception all in one venue and had to be there before the guests arrived, so me, my bridesmaids and my mum and dad took a traditional plain black London Taxi-style cab which the driver put a ribbon on. That taxi then came back in the evening to take me and my new hubby to our hotel at the end of the night. If you are staying at the venue you're getting married in, you might not need transport at all.

If you are getting married at one location and the reception is at another, then you will need transport. So, what are the options? A vintage Rolls Royce? A high-class Mercedes? A stretch Limousine? a sporty Ferrari? Something quirky? There is a plethora of choice available. Below are some of the main options.

The Vintage Car

There is so much choice when it comes to these types of vehicles. Everyone knows Rolls Royce and Bentley, but there are many others. These cars are very photogenic and have plenty of room for a large dress. Vintage cars are nice but they don't like doing long distances. So, check with the company what distance they will do. If you do like a particular vehicle, book it straight away as it's likely to be the only one available!

Stretch Limousine

A stretch limo is great to fit everyone in one go. If you're choosing a British or European limo, they can seat 7 plus the driver. American limos can seat up to 14 or more. So, know your numbers before deciding which is best. Think about where they are getting to. A limo might struggle to get down that narrow country lane or round that tight turn onto the driveway, or up that narrow track.

The Groom's Car

You can hire anything from an Aston Martin to a Bugatti Veyron (which would cost as much to hire as the average wedding in the UK!). There is also the Ferrari, E Type Jaguar and other convertibles. You can hire these as self-drive. You need a totally clean licence and I shouldn't have to add: Do Not Drink and Drive!

The Vintage Bus

This is a great option for transporting all your guests to the reception venue from the ceremony. I love vintage buses and have been on one as a guest and also arranged them for a number of weddings. Again, you have to think about distance and access. If your marquee is on top of a hill, the bus will have to stop at the bottom and you will need to walk. They might also struggle down some narrow lanes, so make sure the company knows the route and they can advise.

Horse and Carriage

Love and marriage go together like a horse and carriage. If you favour the fairy tale wedding or you are the Duke and Duchess of Sussex, this is the perfect way to arrive at your reception venue, castle, or just parade the streets waving at passers-by. The main thing you need to be aware of, if this is the transport for you, is the horses' welfare. Distance is limited to a few miles at most and no steep hills. You might get to keep some manure for your garden afterwards though!

Motorbike

I was coordinating one wedding day and the bride arrived at the reception venue on the back of a motorbike driven by her Dad. She only came up the drive to the venue on it and it was just for the dramatic entrance and photographs. Looked cool though as she held her bouquet.

Other Options

Depending on the location, budget and destination, you can hire hot air balloons, helicopters, replicas of famous cars (Batmobile, Delorian, Del Boys Van, Herbie the Beetle, etc.) or tandem bicycles. You can arrive on elephants, camels and donkeys. If you've got a waterway nearby, you could arrive on a boat. Or you could take a steam train. Choices, choices.

Breakdowns do happen

Breakdowns can occur with both vintage and modern cars. So, it's important to employ a reputable company that will have a professional mechanic check all the cars before they are dispatched and will have back-up vehicles should a breakdown occur. If you hire someone with the one car, or use a family member's vintage car, you could be left with no car at all if it breaks down. Check the car you want to hire looks in good condition and check there is a maintenance record. Also, ask the car company, family friend, or chauffeur, if they have a contingency plan should the worst happen.

What happens if this does happen to you on the morning of your wedding day? With all the stress and emotion running high, you could feel like this has ruined your day. Take a few deep breaths. In the grand scheme of things, it's just a car. Call a taxi, have a laugh about it en route and claim on the insurance after the wedding.

Summary

- Decide if you need transport.
- How many people do you need to transport?
- What is the distance involved?

- What are the roads like?
- What is your budget?
- Pick your transport.
- Factor in travel time and also if there are any roadworks, market days, sporting events, etc., that could mean more time should be allowed.
- Have a contingency plan and a taxi company number.

Wedding Notes

CHAPTER 12
WEDDING ATTIRE

"A man doesn't know what happiness is until he's married. By then it's too late" - Frank Sinatra

The Bridal Gown

Queen Victoria is credited with starting the tradition of the white wedding dress when she married Prince Albert in 1840. Before that, brides usually wore coloured dresses made from heavy silk satin or their Sunday best. Queen Victoria also set another fashion for having bridesmaids carry her train too. While the majority of brides follow tradition with a white or ivory dress, ivory being a better shade for most skin tones than white, not all brides do and it is perfectly acceptable to wear a coloured dress. There are so many designers and choices out there that it can be hard to figure out what you like.

The first stop will probably be your local bridal shop. If you are after a particular designer, then you will need to find a bridal shop that stocks that designer. Once you get to the trying-on process, you need to consider a few things first. Will it suit your shape and is it the right style for your wedding? If you are planning a Gatsby-themed event, you probably won't want a full-skirted princess gown, you will choose something glamorous and sleek. If you are planning a wedding in a field with wellies and hay bales, then a glittery, sequinned, fishtail number will be out of place. Ultimately, you are unlikely to know what suits you straight away, so try on all the different styles for you to see what suits and then you can look for dresses in that style.

What are the main styles available?

Below is an image showing the main five styles that you might hear mentioned and what body type they suit. This will help you narrow down the styles of dresses that will suit your shape. There are other styles available, such as shorter skirts (like a 50's style) or you might prefer a trouser suit or something completely different.

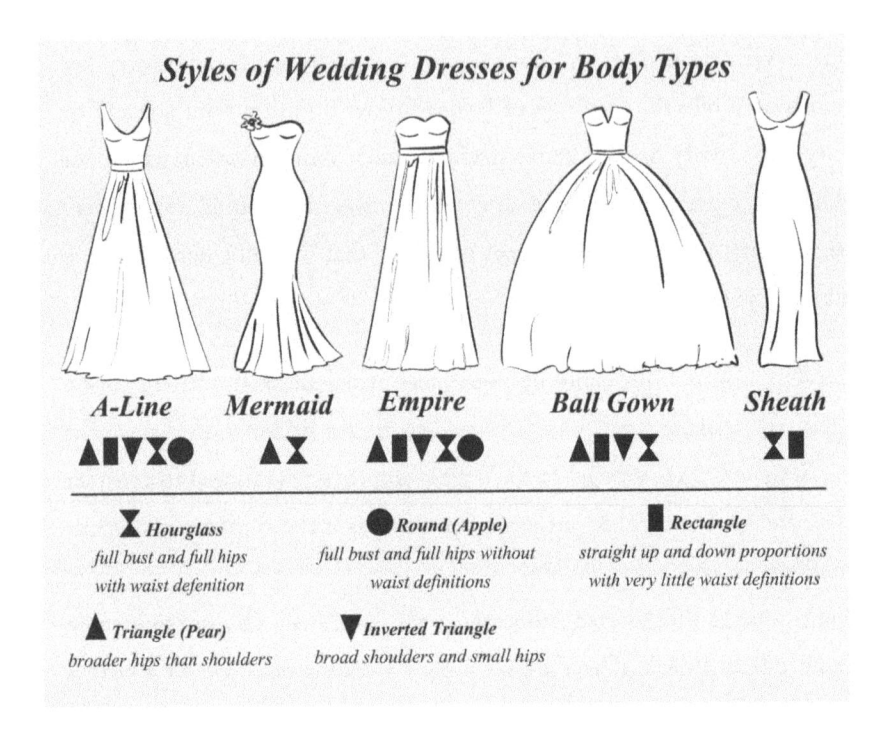

Styles of Wedding Dresses for Body Types

A-Line	Mermaid	Empire	Ball Gown	Sheath
▲■▼✕⬤	▲✕	▲■▼✕⬤	▲■▼✕	✕■

✕ Hourglass — full bust and full hips with waist defenition

⬤ Round (Apple) — full bust and full hips without waist definitions

■ Rectangle — straight up and down proportions with very little waist definitions

▲ Triangle (Pear) — broader hips than shoulders

▼ Inverted Triangle — broad shoulders and small hips

Richard Lill, of Alfred Angelo, offers advice on the Hitched.co.uk blog. When trying your dress on, make sure you sit down in it. You will spend a good chunk of the day sat down so make sure it is comfortable. If the dress is boned, make sure it doesn't dig in. If you are getting married in a church, practice kneeling in it and getting back up again. A hooped underskirt could lift the dress up as you kneel. What about the length? It needs to skim the top of your shoes so you don't trip over it when you walk and you don't want to keep hitching it up all day. What is the venue like? Narrow doorways? A large dress will make getting through them tricky. Lots of stairs? Might be difficult in a tight fishtail dress.

Richard also offers this warning:
"Some brides try a dress on in a shop and then try to find it much cheaper online, but often they are buying counterfeit dresses and they will have no recourse if it doesn't fit or is damaged. If the price of a dress sounds too good to be true, it probably is. Make sure you buy your wedding dress from a reputable bridalwear shop or designer to avoid being conned."
https://www.hitched.co.uk/wedding-planning/bridalwear-articles/how-to-choose-a-wedding-dress/

I would also add: If you don't want company in the toilet with you then make sure you can lift the skirts on your own! Going to be dancing the night away? You will need a dress you can move in, or have a second dress to change into in the evening.

A good bridal shop should be honest with you about what suits you and what doesn't. You will also have your own style and you should embrace that with your bridal gown. If you have a quirky dress sense, then go with it. Pick a dress that is true to you. Also, pick a dress in your budget. Don't go trying on high price-tagged gowns as you might end up falling for a dress you can't afford.

One thing I should say about wedding dresses is to ignore the label size. It bears no relation to normal clothing sizes. I had to order a wedding dress two dress sizes larger than my normal clothes. So, don't pick a smaller one and hope you've lost weight by the fitting. Go with what fits. It can always be taken in if need be.

Don't leave dress shopping too late. If you need a dress that is made to order, then you need to allow at least 6 months. If you are on a budget but you have your eye on a designer gown, why not see if someone is selling one 'preloved' (i.e. second-hand!)? Try sites such as stillwhite.co.uk, Bridal Reloved, Oxfam Bridal and even eBay. If you pick a local seller, they might be happy for you to try before you buy.

I found my perfect dress second-hand on a preloved wedding website. The person was selling a £1200 Ian Stuart gown for £800. It was gorgeous. A fishtailed lace dress in ivory with a cute puddle train and a long-sleeved lace bolero jacket with ostrich feathers around the collar and cuffs. It fitted me well. Then my mother-in-law told me she had seen a dress matching that description in a little bridal shop in Barnsley. I went to check it out and I found the same Ian Stuart dress for £775! My jaw dropped and my eyes sparkled when I saw the row of Ian Stuart gowns before me. So, I obviously tried them all on. It was a hard choice as they were all so fabulous but the original one I saw was 'the one'. So, I bought the new made-to-measure version. I will add that this was in the early noughties and Ian Stuart had not started winning all his 'Bridal Designer of the Year Awards' yet (his first was 2004). You won't find a bridal shop stocking his gowns for less than £1700 I would think these days!

One thing I have noticed on a few weddings, so must be a common occurrence, is that the bride doesn't know or can't remember how the dress hitches up for the evening. Dresses with trains will have some kind of way to lift the train up for the evening and the dancing so it doesn't get dirty or tripped over. I've seen many a bridesmaid or mother of the bride with their head up a skirt trying to figure out how it works.

The Bridesmaids

After the bridal gown, bridesmaid dresses are the next most important. The bridal gown should already be chosen so bridesmaid dresses complement or flatter the bridal dress and look. What is your overall vision for the bridesmaid dresses? Do you see them in identical dresses or mismatched dresses in the same colour scheme? Or the same dresses in different colours? Think about the season you are getting married. Heavy long dresses in the summer won't work, and shorter dresses with no cover-up will be a bit chilly in the winter.

When choosing dresses, make sure you order in plenty of time in case alterations are required. Set a budget for the dresses. If the bridesmaids are contributing to their outfits, make sure you know what they can all afford. Look at the different styles available. Your bridesmaids are likely to be different heights, body shapes and suit different styles. Are there any styles that would suit all of them? If they are all very different, then having mismatched dresses in matching colours is a good option. If you only have one bridesmaid then you don't have to worry about this!

When I got married, it was when Moulin Rouge had just come out at the cinema and I really wanted a red wedding dress like the one Nicole Kidman wore in the film. I couldn't work out what colour to put my bridesmaid in if I wore red. The only colour option seemed to be a light colour and then it might be confusing as to who was the bride and who was the bridesmaid! So, my lucky bridesmaid got to wear a red dress. She did look fabulous in it…(#jealous.)

Arrange a shopping day with your chosen bridesmaids. Try on plenty of dresses. Use this time to find out what styles suit them and just relax and have fun. It might be that not all your bridesmaids know each other and this is a great time for them to get to know each other.

What if one of your bridesmaids announces they are pregnant? By the time of the wedding, they might have just given birth or still be pregnant, so you will need to make sure you factor this into the dress style. Empire line dresses are a good choice and can accommodate a growing bump. Just speak to your bridesmaid and see what is comfortable. On no accounts should you have a Bridezilla moment and accuse the bridesmaid of trying to ruin your wedding or drop her from being your bridesmaid. Seriously, some brides have done this. Don't be one of them.

Once you have chosen the dresses and alterations have been made, have a group fitting. It's another great time to all get together and you can see the completed look for the wedding day. Get the bubbly and tissues ready. It could get emotional!

Don't forget the finishing touches - shoes, bags, wraps, jewellery, hair and make-up. It's a nice idea to give the bridesmaids jewellery as their gift on the morning of the wedding.

The Groom

The groom also needs to look his part and there are plenty of options available too. You need to pick a suit that goes with your wedding theme, location and the time of year. A tweed suit would not be appropriate if you have stated 'black tie' on the wedding invitations. Pastels are better worn at summer weddings.

Hiring a suit is a great option if you want something that you know you won't wear again, such as loud patterns and bright colours. Also, if you are going for a traditional morning suit or tails suit, then you would be better off hiring these.

If you want to splurge, then having a bespoke suit made from scratch will give you exactly what you want and is fitted to perfection. Be prepared to have up to five fittings and the suit could take six months to make, so plan in advance.

TAIL COAT   MORNING COAT   TUXEDO

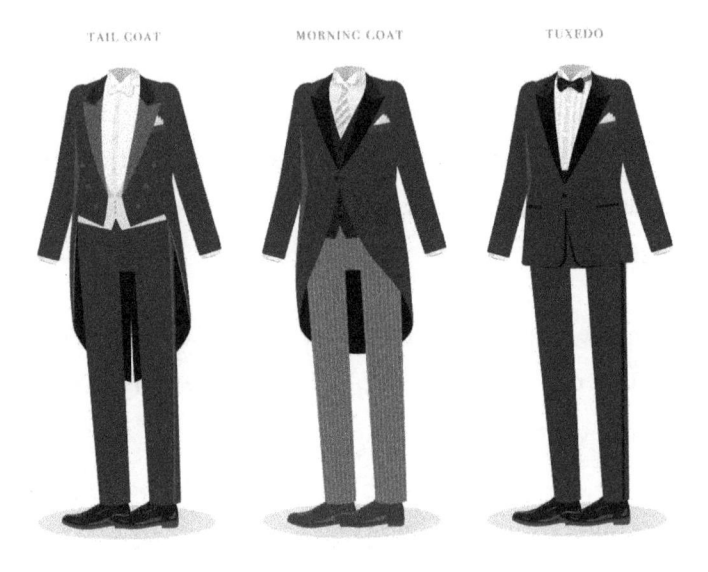

A made-to-measure suit is the in-between option and is made from set patterns but you can pick and choose the style and fabrics and the suit is made to fit.

You need to be comfortable in your suit. You want to look and feel your best as well. Make sure it fits properly, so not too tight when sitting down, or too tight across the chest so that the buttons pull when done up. Make sure it's not too big either. You don't want to look like you borrowed it last minute. And as with the bride, make sure you try on different styles and fits as you may be surprised by what you actually want in the end.

If you are wearing a traditional morning suit with a waistcoat and cravat, it looks good if you have the cravat in the colour scheme of the wedding theme or the colour of the flowers in the bouquet.

Groomsmen

You have a choice whether to dress them the same or different to you. You could also have them dressing in their own unique style if you wanted. As a wedding planner, it helped to have the ushers in the same outfits though so I could find them in a crowd and if a guest or supplier needs to ask a question, they can easily find someone who is part of the wedding party without bothering the bride and groom.

Flower Girls and Page Boys

The main role of the flower girls and page boys are to look pretty and cute. The flower girl's role is often to walk down the aisle sprinkling rose petals and the page boy was to carry the rings. But just having the little darlings walking down the aisle hand in hand can be enough, especially if you think they might be too nervous to do anything else.

Don't shop too early on as little children have a habit of having a growth spurt when you least expect it. Two months is about the right time to go shopping for outfits for younger members of the wedding party. For flower girls, a mini version of a white or ivory dress is perfect. You can always add a splash of colour with a satin sash. For the page boys, they are usually dressed as a mini version of the groom, complete with a waistcoat and tie. Or for extra cuteness, a bowtie.

Wedding Notes

CHAPTER 13
HAIR AND MAKE-UP

"The beauty of marriage is not always seen from the very beginning—but rather as love grows and develops over time." —Fawn Weaver

One part of the wedding day I was rarely privy too was the bride and her bridal party getting ready and the hair and makeup. On the morning of the wedding, unless the ceremony and/or reception was in the same venue, I would be elsewhere getting the venues ready. I obviously have my own experience of getting ready on my wedding day, but I did my own makeup. Hair was done professionally though.

Hair

If you're anything like me, and most people aren't, you probably spend very little time doing your hair. OK, so I'm probably in the minority of women who just wash my hair and leave it to air dry and then stick it in a ponytail. But if you are someone not used to styling your hair, then you'll need to look for wedding hair inspiration. Again, wedding magazines, websites, Pinterest, and Instagram will all have plenty of ideas.

Pick a style that compliments your wedding dress. A sleek up-do looks fabulous for a black-tie wedding. A loose, braided effect is perfect for a relaxed boho wedding. The internet is awash with images of hairstyles for all wedding styles and length of hair.

A hairstylist will work with you before your wedding day to try out different styles and see which you prefer. The wedding trial is essential to see your favourite style in action or to change it if it is not working for you. It should be scheduled approximately four to six weeks before the wedding. They have years of experience and will be able to give you a style that will last all day and look fabulous in the photos. Remember to take any hair accessories to your trial so that the stylist can work with your veil or tiara, etc.

In the six months before your wedding day, start a hair maintenance routine to get your hair in tip-top condition. If you are planning to colour your hair, then make sure you start early and try to avoid a drastic colour change or attempting it yourself at home if it is the first time you've done it.

Avoid attempting anything too drastic a week before the wedding. A simple cut and colour three weeks before will be enough. You don't want to have to rethink your hairstyle at short notice because you've cut too much off.

Makeup

Natalie Willingham, a makeup artist of over ten years, has seen it all on wedding mornings and nothing surprises her anymore. Here, she gives her tips on choosing a makeup artist, how to get the most from your trial and what to expect on the big day.

Choosing a Makeup Artist

- Ask friends who have recently married for a recommendation.
- Ask your photographer, venue, florist, etc. for recommendations. They will work with people on a regular basis and can help steer you in the right direction.
- Do an internet search of makeup artists in your area or venue's area. Most artists will travel but it is worth checking this before booking. Use keywords (glam, natural, vegan, vintage) to ensure you get the right people.
- Each artist will have a signature style. Spend time looking through each artist's website and social media channels to get a feel for this. Check out the real brides and not just the styled inspirational shoots.
- Once you have a shortlist of artists whose style most reflects how you want to look on your big day, give them a call.
- The relationship with your makeup artist is crucial. You need to trust them with how you want to look and feel on your wedding day, so it's important to find someone who understands this.
- Good people get booked early, often one to two years in advance. So, leaving it until six months before your wedding may be too late to work with your makeup artist of choice.
- Brides often underestimate how long hair and makeup takes, so bear this in mind when choosing the number of bridesmaids you want, or selecting a service time. It's quite normal for Makeup Artists to start work at 6 am, even with a 1 pm service time.

Bridal Trial

Natalie always recommends having a trial in advance of your big day to ensure your wedding morning is stress-free. She recommends scheduling your trial six to twelve weeks before your wedding day. By this point, you should have your dress, selected accessories and a good idea of how you want to look. Where possible, schedule your trial before your dress fitting so you can see how the whole look works together. Whilst it may be tempting to try a completely new look, you should ensure that you incorporate aspects of your personality so that your partner recognises you at the end of the aisle. There's little point in having a strong makeup look if you never usually wear it.

Pinterest has a great source of images and will show the makeup artist what you love but also what you really don't like. If you are not sure, then trust your makeup artist to create a look specifically for you. They will have a lot of experience working with different brides and will keep an eye on the catwalk to ensure they keep up to date with current trends, which can then be incorporated into stunning bridal looks. Be realistic about what can be achieved. Your skin, bone structure and hair will be different from the photos you share. Often, these photos have been retouched, false hair has been used, and models have been primped and preened in between shots. The looks are not created for longevity which is what is needed for a wedding day. Use images for inspiration and create a look for you that is inspired by the photos but is 100% you.

Natalie usually suggests that the brides wear a white or light-coloured top to their trial. The combination of light and the white colour will provide the most accurate example of how your makeup and hair will look on the day. If you don't have a white top, then a white towel or pillowcase will work just as well.

Lighting is really important. Lighting at home or in hotels can cast shadows and yellow tones, which can change the look and colour of your makeup. More makeup artists are bringing their own lights on location to ensure they can control this.

Bring any accessories with you to your trial as these can also affect the look of your hair and makeup. Strong accessories may need fuller lashes or stronger colours to emphasise your look. If you haven't decided, then bring a couple of options with you so you can see which works best.

Be honest about how you look and feel. Remain open to ideas. Natalie has created looks specifically as requested by a client but then felt it wasn't right and so they have gone back to the drawing board and created something entirely different. Remember, this is their job, so any feedback they get is really useful and helps them to help you achieve the look you've always wanted.

Talk to your Makeup Artist about whether or not to tan. Consider clothing in hot weather to avoid tan lines showing in your wedding dress. If you have tattoos, speak to your Makeup Artist in advance if you are considering having these covered. Tattoo cover takes time and specific products and your makeup artist will need to consider this prior to your wedding day.

Wedding Morning

- The makeup artist will check out the space she will be expected to work in. Usually, all that is required is a table, chair and a plug socket near a window, but if there is a mirror as well, that's fantastic.
- The makeup artist will usually check the running order with the bride in case there have been any issues. Wedding prep is planned to the exact minute so there is little time for error. Losing twenty minutes of styling time as someone has gone to get breakfast can make the difference to feeling stressed or relaxed.
- Bridal prep can get very warm with lots of people coming and going and styling tools being used. Remember to check if your room has fans or air conditioning available.
- Don't forget to offer your makeup artist refreshments. They are often stood working without a break for six or more hours. If you want them to perform their best, keep them hydrated.
- Avoid changing your mind about styles on the morning of your wedding, these have not been trialled and it all adds additional stress.

SECTION 2

2-6 MONTHS BEFORE 'I DO'

CHAPTER 14
STATIONERY

"What's the best way to get your husband to remember your anniversary? Get married on his birthday"
- Cindy Garner

Save the date cards, invitations, RSVP cards, order of service, menus, table numbers, place names - that's a lot of stationery (not stationary - which is what a car is when parked).

Save the Date Cards

These can be sent out a year in advance to tell people to save the date and not book a holiday. These are more important if you are having your wedding during a time when people will likely be on their holidays. They are not essential and, for most people, you will have probably told them all about it already.

Invitations

So much choice is available. From handmade designs to bespoke digital printing, eco-designs, off-the-shelf designs, or printable downloads. You could design your own stationery to get printed. If you get a chance to go to a wedding fayre, you can see examples. Most companies will be able to send free samples of their work. Again, Pinterest will have loads of examples.

How many do you need? You don't need one per guest! If you have 100 guests and the majority are couples, then you'll need 50. If some are a family of 3 or more, you'll need less. Some people will need invitations for the full day and some will need invitations for the evening only. You probably don't need to send invitations to your parents or children. Depends how much contact you usually have with them.

Invitations are often sent with maps, hotel options, a gift list, and menu choices, for example, so they can get a bit bulky. Some couples choose to include an RSVP card and some don't.

One couple had wedding invitations that were like a cheque book. They had a hand-drawn picture of the venue on the front and then inside were perforated pages with the invite, directions, menu choice/RSVP card and hotel option. Other couples have had a wedding website with all the details and the guests could log on and RSVP on the site. This saves on paper! Back before people were savvy with websites, I knew some couples who sent the information on CD-Roms!

You can easily find example wording online, but the invitation would include who's hosting, the request to come to the wedding, the names of the couple, the date and time and location.

A couple of examples:
If it's the parents of the bride and a formal wedding, you might use:

> Mr and Mrs Smith request the pleasure of the company of (insert guest names) at the marriage of their daughter (name) to (insert name of groom) on (date and time) at (ceremony location) and afterwards at (reception

location).

If the couple are hosting and it's a less formal occasion:

(Couples names) invite you to celebrate their marriage on...etc.

Table Names

The easy option is table numbers but you can use names instead. Here, you can personalise the tables with something you are interested in - favourite book titles, holiday destinations, bands you have seen, etc. Some couples have used locations of where they have lived or where guests are from to name the tables.

It's quite easy to print out the name or number and put it in a frame to stand on the table.

Place Names

This is important if you are wanting your guests to sit in certain places on tables. These can be simple folded cards with the name of the guest on, either printed or hand-written. If they can sit anywhere on their assigned table then you won't need these. As mentioned in Chapter 3, if there are menu choices or dietary requirements, add these to the back of the cards.

Menus

I think it's a nice touch to prepare a menu and put it on the table. It gets the guests excited about what is to come. Or forewarns them if it's something they don't like!

Order of Service

This is more likely to be required during a religious ceremony where there are sermons and hymns. These can be added to the order of service and everyone knows where they are in the proceedings.

Table Plans

These are discussed in chapter 15.

Other Items

You may want personalised stickers to go on wedding favours. You can also buy personalised wrapping paper or gift bags and tags for the gifts.

CHAPTER 15
PREPARING THE SEATING PLAN

"If I get married, I want to be very married."
- Audrey Hepburn

Ah, the fun bit! (Not.) Prepare for stress levels to rise and to deal with disagreements. It's hard enough choosing who to invite and then you need to decide where to sit them. What if some guests don't get on? What if some take offence at where they are seated? It is worth talking to your close family and wedding party before the day if you feel that some people might get upset about where they are sitting or who they will or won't be sat with. If you know your Uncle Bob and Uncle Joe don't get on, sit them at opposite sides of the room. If the partner of your chief bridesmaid is really shy and doesn't know anyone, then sit them together at another table. So, this can take more logistical planning than the Moon landings.

So, let's start with the Top Table.

Top Table

Traditionally, this is a long table seating the couple, the parents, the best man and the chief bridesmaid (or matron of honour). However, as families are getting increasingly more diverse or people are getting married older and there may be children of the couple involved, this top table arrangement just won't work. You might want a round top table and sit in the middle of the room and have your guests' tables around the outside. You might have so many people wanting to sit on the top table that you do away with it altogether. Sit yourselves at a table for two and enjoy each other's company. Or set yourselves settings on different tables and move between courses. If you're having a relaxed wedding without a set seating plan, then the top table is a non-issue.

So, how to go about seating everyone else?

Firstly, you need your guest replies. No point trying to fit in the difficult great-aunt if she isn't actually coming. Then you group your family and friends. So, you will want close family on the tables near the top table, and your closest friends near too.

What we tried to do when I got married was to make sure everyone knew at least two or three people on each table. So, for example, the cousins sat with some of our friends or cousins on the other side of the family and not necessarily with their parents. Then aunts and uncles sat with other aunts and uncles, etc. There is usually one table which ends up being 'everyone leftover' or the 'rowdy group'. But do try to make it look like that hasn't happened! If there are older children at the wedding, say, young teens, they could sit together away from their parents. Or you could have a kids table.

The Seating Plan

This is the way everyone finds out where they are sitting. The simple way is a board stood on an easel at the entrance with the Table Name/Number and a list of the people underneath. These can be large chalkboards or A2 printed to match the stationery. You can print each Table out and stick to some pretty paper and put in a large ornate frame.

Other ways I've seen is having a table with all the place cards on it in alphabetical order and the name card has the table number on.

A complicated but interesting version at one wedding had guest names in two columns down each side of the board. The tables were in the middle of the board and each name was attached to the relevant table with different coloured wool and pins! It looked really spectacular and complicated and obviously a lot of work had gone into it.

Pinterest will have lots of ideas. I'm not affiliated with Pinterest by the way - I just wish it was around when I was getting married! Instagram will also be a source of ideas.

Wedding Notes

CHAPTER 16
WEDDING TRADITIONS

"We are all a little weird and life's a little weird. And when we find someone whose weirdness is compatible with ours, we join up with them and fall in mutual weirdness and call it love." — Dr. Seuss

In this chapter, we will look at some wedding etiquette and traditions and why some of them are there. It's good to do something different and shakes things up, but sometimes following a tradition makes things a bit easier as you're not reinventing the wheel so to speak. I personally love weddings that are different.

Something old, something new, something borrowed, something blue

I'm sure you will have heard this phrase mentioned before. But where has this little rhyming tradition come from? According to blog site, The Knot (theknot.com), it derives from the Old English rhyme, "Something Olde, Something New, Something Borrowed, Something Blue, A Sixpence in your Shoe"—which names the four good-luck objects (plus a sixpence to bring prosperity) a bride should include somewhere in her wedding outfit or carry with her on her wedding day.

Something Old was traditionally included to ward off the evil eye and protect any future children the couple might have. But generally, this now represents continuity and a couple might use this tradition to wear a piece of jewellery or item belonging to an older relative.

Something New is optimism for the future. It is a new chapter in the couple's life, so something new represents that. Anything new the couple is wearing can tick this box, such as the bridal gown, veil or shoes.

Something Borrowed brings the couple good luck. Borrowing from a happily married friend or relative was said to ensure that their good fortune will rub off on them too. The old-fashioned superstition urged the bride to borrow the undergarments of a happily married friend with healthy children (to promote fertility). Not sure I would wear a friend's underwear though! But you can borrow anything if you would like to observe this tradition (*I borrowed a friend's wedding shoes, although now I write this, I think I still have them!*).

Something Blue was also meant to deflect the evil eye and also stands for purity, love and fidelity. A traditional something blue was often a blue garter worn under the wedding dress. You don't have to wear something blue to ward off the evil spirits, you could include it in other parts of the wedding such as adding blue flowers to your bouquet or a blue ribbon to your invitations.

(https://www.theknot.com/content/wedding-traditions-the-meaning-of-something-old)

Walking Down the Aisle

It's not essential to be walked down the aisle and 'given away' anymore. I think this is a tradition falling by the wayside as couples choose to either walk down alone or together. Sometimes the bridesmaids walk behind the bride, sometimes they head down the aisle first.

I did one wedding where the couple had an awesome punk-rock wedding and they each came down the aisle to their own song, through clouds of dry ice, with lights set to music. It was a dramatic entrance and they felt like they were the stars of their own rock concert. Certainly one of the best entrances I've seen.

Check out YouTube for some unusual entrances. Make an entrance anyway you like I say!

Chimney Sweeps

There is a tradition that it is good luck to shake the hand of a chimney sweep on your wedding day and I have coordinated weddings where a chimney sweep was hired to wait outside the ceremony room to shake the couple's hand. But where has this tradition come from? According to Curioushistory.com, it dates back to when a chimney sweep saved the life of King George II:

"It was the 17th century, when one fine day, King George II was riding his horse on the street of London. Unexpectedly, a big dog came in his path and scared the horse. The horse lost its control because of fear and started jumping restlessly. King George II also lost his control on the reins. There were many people on the street who were witnessing this incident but no one came out to help the king. Then suddenly a courageous chimney sweep appeared and helped the king by grabbing the horse. This heroic act saved the King's life. It was the moment when King George II gratefully declared chimney sweep as the sign of future success. From then, chimney sweeps were regarded as a sign of good luck and success in England."

The Line-Up

This is where the bride and groom and the parents line up and greet every guest as they enter the room for the wedding breakfast. It takes ages and most people just want to get seated and fed. But it's an option if that's the only way you think you'll get to talk to all your guests during the day. I've not done many weddings where the couple have had a line-up.

Cutting the Cake

This tradition stems from the time when, historically, the bride would make the first cut to ensure the marriage would be blessed with children.

Horseshoes

The giving of horseshoes to a bride is a long-standing tradition. Well before Christian times, a horseshoe was thought to represent a crescent moon and was, therefore, a very potent fertility charm (this theme cropping up again). In Victorian times, the tradition was established as a way of bringing good luck to the newlyweds for the duration of their lives together. The horseshoe has to be held upright as, otherwise, all the luck will run out.

There is also the superstition that the buttonholes also need to be pinned upright (until at least after the ceremony) to preserve the good luck for the couple.

Throwing Confetti

The throwing of confetti or rice is another tradition thought to increase good luck and fertility. There's a theme here!

Wedding Notes

CHAPTER 17
THE SPEECHES

"Weddings are a marvellous excuse for a big party, and today is no exception. We have a lot of people here today – grandparents, aunts, uncles, cousins, friends… and a handful of people I recognise."

Traditionally, it is the father-of-the-bride first (as it used to be him who paid for the wedding, therefore, he would speak first), then the groom, then the best man would round off with some funny anecdotes about the groom. Sometimes a religious leader will also give a speech. I've been to some weddings where the Rabbi, Iman or the Vicar who gave the service has spoken during the speeches.

These days, you will just as likely see the mother of the bride, the bride and the chief bridesmaid giving a speech. It's not all about the men speaking. Obviously, if this is a civil partnership, there will be two brides or two grooms. So, you can choose to speak or not speak as is your choice. As long as someone greets everyone, people who need to be thanked are thanked and sentiments of love are given, then anything goes. You could even have an open mic session (if you're feeling brave!). All I would say is try to keep to under 10 minutes per speech. I've been to some weddings where they were still going on as evening guests arrived and they can end up feeling awkward arriving during the speeches. Try not to do the speeches in front of mirrors as it makes it very difficult for a videographer or the photographer to not be seen in the footage or photos.

So, what needs to be included at a minimum during the speeches? I'm going to talk *traditionally* here - but you can substitute any family member, or bride for the groom, chief bridesmaid for best man, etc.

The father of the bride - or the equivalent speech opener - needs to welcome all the guests, they need to thank all the helpers and suppliers, talk about how wonderful a day it is and then say some lovely things about the bride.

The groom's main role here is to thank all the guests and say wonderful things about his bride. He also needs to thank the wedding party (bridesmaids, ushers, flower girls, etc.) and then the couple will hand out gifts to them and the parents (usually) or anyone who deserves a gift on the day. This speech will likely touch on family members who couldn't be there. This is the tearjerker speech.

The best man is traditionally the last to speak and his role is to accept thanks on behalf of the bridesmaids (if one of those isn't speaking), read out messages from guests who couldn't be there and give a couple of funny (emphasis on funny) anecdotes about the groom, how they met, etc. I've heard dozens and dozens of best man speeches. Some have been hilarious and spot-on, some have really missed the mark in both length and content, some have been far too rude for Grandma's ears (these have been very funny though!), and some were just long and boring. I've seen double acts, PowerPoints and quizzes given. All this depends on your confidence as a speaker. If you're not confident, my advice is to keep it to the main points, don't get drunk before the speech and fail to say anything at all, and have it written down. If in doubt, raise your glass, make a toast to the happy couple and tell everyone to hit the bar (as long as you are the last to speak that is!).

Master of Ceremonies/Toastmaster

You might want to designate someone to be Master of Ceremonies, someone who is happy to use a microphone and make announcements throughout the day. It can be a hired Toastmaster or a family member or friend who likes the sound of their own voice. They need to announce the couple into the wedding breakfast, announce the speeches and anything else that might need an announcement such as cutting the cake.

I did one wedding which had a famous guest, and he was the Master of Ceremonies and also gave a funny speech too. He was obviously used to speaking in public, being famous for his TV work, but he also didn't steal the limelight from the couple. But not everyone is comfortable with a microphone, and that could equally apply to one of the wedding party assigned the role as your wedding day coordinator.

At one wedding, even though I make it clear I am a behind the scenes coordinator, I had a microphone thrust into my hands and was asked to announce the speeches and the cutting of the cake, in the middle of a large dance floor surrounded by 250 people. I had to turn on the confidence and announce each speaker, which went fine until the best man, who had mysteriously disappeared and left me standing there!

CHAPTER 18
CHILDREN AT WEDDINGS

"When we are in love, we are open to all that life has to offer with passion, excitement, and acceptance."
– John Lennon

If you don't have children yet, you may be wanting to keep the wedding a no-children zone. You may be worried that there will be kids running amok, knocking over the cake or crying during the speeches. This is obviously a personal choice and if you are booking an expensive wedding and the catering for the children is almost the same cost as an adult, then excluding children can keep costs down.

When I got married, I had lots of young cousins and we invited them to the day, but then kept the evening as adults only. So, my aunties and uncles with kids left before the evening. In the end, I don't think it would have mattered if they had stayed and I'm not sure why we made that decision in the first place now.

If you have children, you might have been on the end of invitations where your children were not included in a wedding invite. This can be disappointing and you can end up feeling affronted that your darlings are not invited.

This has personally happened and we were the proud parents of a new baby and not at the stage where he could be left, so we had to turn down the invite and we felt hurt that he wasn't invited. As they got older, the reverse was true and the kids were invited and we left them with the grandparents so we could have a day out child-free!

So, think about who you are inviting and what it would mean to you and to them if they couldn't be at your wedding because they couldn't get childcare. Personally, I love seeing all the children at weddings, they have such a fun time and it's a great family occasion.

How do you handle the situation though? Charlotte Grainger, writing for Brides.com, offers the following advice:

If you have close family and friends with children, they may find banning children at the wedding accommodating and rude and there is the inconvenience of organising childcare. So, what are the options?

- Can you compromise? Only have children within your family present so not to upset relatives? Or if your best friend, one of the bridesmaids, has children, could she bring them?
- Be clear about what you have decided and communicate it. You need to let guests know children are invited if they are, so include the children on the invite. If children are not invited, then make it clear. Be honest but don't over-explain your reason.
- If only select children can come, you need to let guests know which ones. Be aware that some guests who couldn't bring children may be unhappy when they arrive on the day to see some children, especially if they were told 'no children'.
- Let the parents know that the duty of care lies with them and you, the couple, are not responsible.

https://www.brides.com/story/inviting-children-to-wedding-rules-etiquette

Whatever you decide, it is your day and you should plan accordingly. As long as you are open and honest early on, most people will understand.

Catering for Children

If you are having a wedding where you know there will be lots of children, it is a good idea to discuss this with the caterer. Especially if you are having 'fine dining' style food, as many children won't be impressed and it's also a waste of food and money if they don't eat it. So, prepare a menu they would like.

Set up an activity table or area for the children. This can be a simple area with colouring and paper craft activities. If you have a separate room available, you could hire some soft play equipment or provide board games. Groups of children together can be loud though, so a separate area, away from the speeches would be best! Or they can have individual activities on the table, or books (depending on the ages) to keep them occupied.

Children's Entertainment

You can hire bouncy castles or oversized outdoor games (the adults love these as well!). Sometimes your entertainment can double up, e.g. your magician during the wedding breakfast could do a thirty-minute kids show in another room for the children during the speeches. Or you can hire a dedicated entertainer for this purpose.

CHAPTER 19
PERSONALISING YOUR WEDDING

"I would rather share one lifetime with you than face all the ages of this world alone."
– Arwen, The Fellowship of the Ring (J.R.R. Tolkien)

This is where you come up with all the little details, extras and personal touches that make your wedding different to everyone else's wedding. Or at least makes everyone say "Oh that was so you two!"

This can come in the form of the wedding vows, the readings, or the wedding favours on the tables.

Writing Vows

If you are having a ceremony where you have the option of writing your own wedding vows, then this is a lovely way of personalising your ceremony. These are unique to you and your partner. Writing your own vows costs nothing and adds a special touch to the ceremony that you and your guests will remember. This can seem quite daunting at first but you can start by simply making a list of why you love this person, how they make you feel, how they make life better and what your hopes are for your future together. There is plenty of inspiration online. Another way to write a vow is to use a sentence or two from literature or a song, then add how you feel and then finish with a vow. If you are opting for a humanist ceremony, then the celebrant will be able to assist with writing your vows.

Questions to help you write your own vows:

- What is the greatest thing about the person you're marrying?
- When did you know you were in love/wanted to get married?
- What does marriage mean to you?
- What will change about your relationship?
- What will stay the same?
- What is your favourite memory of your partner?
- How does your partner make you feel?
- What are your dreams for the future?

Readings and Songs

You can also include songs and readings that are special to you. If you are having a civil ceremony, you will not be able to use any religious songs or readings, so do check with your registrar when you have chosen readings and songs so they can confirm they are allowed. There are plenty of online resources to help you choose readings for your ceremony. If you are having a humanist celebrant, they will be able to assist with personalising your ceremony. The   is the reading my sister-in-law read when I got married:

An Apache wedding blessing

Now you will feel no rain,
for each of you will be shelter for the other.
Now you will feel no cold,
for each of you will be warmth to the other.

Now there will be no loneliness,
for each of you will be companion to the other.
Now you are two persons,
But there is only one life before you.
May beauty surround you both in the journey ahead and through all the years.
May happiness be your companion to the place where the river meets the sun.
And may your days be good and long upon the earth.

Wedding Favours

These are the little gifts that are placed at each guest's place at the tables. Traditionally, it was a little mesh bag of sugared almonds. I have also seen scratch cards, packets of seeds, charity donations in the guests' name, little succulent plants, personalised miniature bottles of whisky, personalised tubes of sweets, and objects collected from the couple's travels. This is a great way to personalise your wedding as you can choose a little gift that is from the heart and also adds another decorative element on the table. One wedding I coordinated, the couple had collected over 100 mugs of various styles that the guests would use for their tea and coffee but could also keep afterwards. Just remember that if you are making your own wedding favours, give yourself plenty of time. You can also rope in your bridesmaids to help if necessary.

SECTION 3

1 MONTH BEFORE 'I DO'

CHAPTER 20
THE FINAL WEEKS

"I love being married. It's so great to find that one special person you want to annoy for the rest of your life."
– Rita Rudner

This chapter covers the final few weeks before the wedding day and sorting out those finishing touches. If I was doing on-the-day coordination, I would be involved from about six weeks before the wedding day. In this section, I will focus on what you need to do in those final four to six weeks. If you have hired a coordinator for the day, then they should be doing this for you. If not, hopefully, the information in this section will be useful and will help keep you on top of the organisation.

- Contact all your suppliers to confirm the details and timings with them. You might have booked some suppliers almost a year beforehand. It's definitely a good idea to contact them six weeks before the wedding day to check everything is still ok. If you discover a problem now, there is still plenty of time to fix it.

- Give your suppliers a phone number of someone who will be able to speak with them on the day if there are any problems. If you have an on-the-day coordinator, they will be the contact on the day. Otherwise, delegate one of the wedding party.

- Let your suppliers know when the ceremony is, so they don't try and call when that is happening.
- Make a contact sheet for all the suppliers. Include the contact name who will be there on the day and their mobile number. Make sure this list is given to the responsible person on the day.
- Prepare a wedding day timeline. I have included an example at the back of the book. At a minimum, it should include the time, the activity and the location. You might want to add additional information in another column such as who is responsible for an activity (e.g. if someone needs to collect the grandparents on the morning, put that on the list and who is responsible for that).
- Distribute the wedding timeline with the wedding party and the suppliers so everyone is working from the same timings.
- Compile final numbers, guest dietary requirements/menu choices and give these to the caterer.
- Prepare the seating plan based on your final numbers. Don't get the seating plan finished until you know the final numbers.

I prepared the seating plan board for a couple once. At least three times after I finalised it, they came back to me with changes. The final one was the night before the wedding day. To say I was not amused was an understatement.

- Organise everything for each table. If you have made your own place cards, table names, and other items for the tables, put these together in a separate box or bag for each table. This makes it quicker and easier for

setting up, especially if someone has to do it the morning of the wedding.
- If you have children at the wedding, you may want to prepare activity sets for them to be placed at the table.
- Dress fitting! This will happen in the final few weeks.
- Collect your bridal gown - usually 2 weeks before the wedding day.
- Collect the men's suits - usually a few days before the wedding day if hiring them.
- Pay all your final invoices.

Wedding Rehearsals

Some venues, especially churches, will organise a wedding rehearsal. This is a great time to get the wedding party together and run through the proceedings of the day. You will get a chance to walk through the ceremony, discuss the timings, allocate jobs and then go for dinner afterwards where you can finally relax as you know everything is ready and everyone knows what they should be doing.

Take time out from the planning

Sometimes the planning can take over your life and there will come a point when you won't remember what you used to do before you started planning your wedding. You need to take time away from planning or thinking about your wedding day. You don't want to become a wedding bore and it be your only topic of conversation when you meet up with friends.

Planning can also take a toll on your relationships with your partner, especially when it gets to the guest list, the advice from the in-laws and well-meaning family members, and arguments over whether there should be a free bar or to show the crucial World Cup match, which was inconveniently scheduled for halfway through the wedding breakfast.

So, take time away. Go on a break together or plan a night out where the wedding is off-limits as a conversation point. Even going to the cinema will take you both away from the wedding planning (just make sure you go and see a film that doesn't involve weddings!).

CHAPTER 21
THE WEDDING DAY

"There is no more lovely, friendly and charming relationship, communion or company, than a good marriage."
— Martin Luther

So, all your meticulous planning comes down to this one day. The day you say 'I do' to your partner! If you have planned everything well, then everyone should know what their roles or jobs are on the day (let's hope the groomsmen are not too hungover to hand out orders of service at the church). Hand over the timings to someone responsible as this is the time to enjoy getting ready and enjoy your day.

If you have a wedding day coordinator, and they are so worth the money, then they will take charge of everything and will make sure that your wedding party are doing their duties and that all the suppliers are where they should be. They'll also be rushing around in the background dealing with issues that you won't even know about (remember the tablecloth, chairs, tableware incidents? The couples didn't notice at all!). Dealing with the band arriving, discussing electrics, organising caterers, cutting the cake up, holding babies and changing nappies during the speeches (yes, done that too!). You won't realise what's going on when you have a good wedding coordinator as you will be left to enjoy your day. If you don't have a coordinator, someone will need to be the central contact for all problems - usually the best man or one of the bridesmaids will take on this role. But if you've followed the advice in Chapter 20, then someone will already be assigned this role.

Getting Ready

This is a time to be pampered and have someone do your makeup and hair. You'll have your bridesmaids with you and it can be a fun time getting ready. Make sure you have given yourself plenty of time so you don't feel rushed.

Have something to eat! You might not feel hungry now but that wedding breakfast is a long way off. Leave your dress until the last minute to put on.

Natalie Willingham, as a makeup artist of over ten years, offers her experience of getting ready on the wedding morning:

The person dressing the bride is normally first in the running order, with the bride second to last. This means that once the bride is styled, she doesn't have to wait for too long before she needs to dress. Flower girls are normally the last to style, to avoid having to keep them tidy for too long. Everyone should ideally be ready to dress one hour before you need to leave for your ceremony. This allows time for the photographer to take any bridal portraits and then leave to get to the venue on time. Before you have your makeup applied, remember to brush your teeth and have the lipstick you want to wear ready.

Same for the men, get ready in good time and get to the ceremony venue in plenty of time. The photographer will probably have arranged to do the groomsmen group photos before the ceremony.

The Ceremony

As mentioned in previous chapters, you need to plan your journey. You don't want to keep your partner waiting too long for you to arrive. You cannot be late for registrars as they often have a few weddings in one day and may need to be elsewhere after yours. You need to be there fifteen to twenty minutes beforehand to see the registrar before the ceremony.

I did one wedding where the bride was almost an hour late! This played havoc with the groom's nerves and also set the rest of the day's proceedings back.

With today's technology, it is now possible to live stream your wedding to people who cannot attend the ceremony. You might need permission from the venue to do this, especially if it is a public space.

Take it slowly walking down the aisle. Don't rush this moment. Look around you at the guests. Take the whole thing in and give the photographer and videographer time to film you. It doesn't matter whether you send the bridesmaids down the aisle before or after you. This is just personal preference.

The ceremony should be quite straightforward as the person taking the ceremony will be leading this and will tell you what to say and when to say it. Not often are there surprises during a ceremony. I've not had a 'Stop the wedding!' moment or the congregation bringing out instruments like in the film *Love Actually*, but I have seen some unusual things.

I did one wedding where the surprise in the ceremony (for the guests) was going to be an owl flying down the aisle and delivering the rings to the groom (I kid you not, this is a thing). One member of the congregation was terrified by owls and she did have to be warned in advance to sit on an outside edge away from the aisle. It was a good job she had spotted the van before going in and she came to see me about it before the ceremony, so at least she was forewarned and we didn't have a guest screaming hysterically during the service!

After the Ceremony

This is usually a good time for the photographer to take the larger group photos before the guests dash off to the drinks reception. The photographer will then use the time before the wedding breakfast to do most of the couple's shots and smaller group photos.

There might be items, such as floral arrangements, that need moving from the ceremony to the reception venue, so make sure someone is in charge of this.

The Wedding Breakfast

Once all the guests have been rounded up and herded to their tables (this can sometimes take up to 30 minutes, especially if they have dispersed over a wide area), someone will announce the couple into the room, everyone will clap and cheer as they sit down and then the caterer can take over.

The caterer will serve the top table first and then usually in table number order. It's quite likely that the first few tables may have finished before the last table has their food.

If you're having a buffet or street food, or catering that the guests need to queue for, you need to make sure there is some order to the proceedings. Assign a member of the wedding party with a microphone to call out table numbers as the queue goes down. This is especially important if they have to go outside and it is raining! Hopefully, the caterer will have thought of this and have a tent or gazebo to cover the buffet station.

The speeches may occur before, during or after the meal. Again, someone needs to be on hand with the microphone to announce each speaker and hand them the microphone.

After the Wedding Breakfast

If there is no change to the room layout, the day flows straight into the evening part of the wedding day and you will have timed everything right so that the evening guests turn up after the wedding breakfast has been cleared away and the speeches finished.

Sometimes the room will need to be reorganised. If you are having a ceilidh, the tables need to be moved back, for example. Assign a team to help do this quickly. You may find that moving guests from their seats will take longer than you think!

During this time, it's a lovely idea to get away for a few minutes and just be alone, just the two of you to reflect on the day.

The Evening

The dancing usually kicks off after the first dance. This can be a shuffle round the floor for a few minutes or you can choreograph a routine. Check out YouTube for some awesome first dances and routines from the wedding party.

At my wedding, we performed a choreographed cha-cha-cha to Barry White's My First, My Last, My Everything. My husband hated the dance lessons and didn't really want to do it on the day. But I talked him round and we removed a section from the middle that he wasn't comfortable with (compromising, very important) and the guests loved it as no one expected us to launch into a routine. This was before the days of YouTube, so we felt like trendsetters!

Once the evening has started and the party is in full swing, there is very little left to do but enjoy yourself and dance the night away. Then it's off to your hotel room to reflect on the amazing, well planned day you had. You got hitched without a hitch!

The perfect start to your married life together.

CHAPTER 22
FINAL THOUGHTS FROM THE WEDDING PLANNER

"A marriage doesn't have to be perfect, but you can be perfect for each other." – Jessica Simpson

As a wedding planner and on-the-day coordinator, I have seen many amazing weddings and also seen things that the couple hadn't got quite right. Usually, it was all sorted during the day and the couple and the guests would be none the wiser. But if you don't have an on-the-day coordinator running around in the background smoothing things out, you will want to take note of these final words of advice:

1. Never assume anything!
2. Communicate. So important.
3. Double-check you have hired everything you need. Draw out a plan of the venue and where everything will go and check you have all the tables, tablecloths and chairs you need.
4. Do have a wedding day timetable. If the ceremony is at 1 pm at the church, don't plan the drinks reception to start at 2 pm when the ceremony takes forty-five minutes, there's photographs to follow and the reception venue is a thirty-minute drive away.
5. Likewise, plan getting to the ceremony venue, work back how long it takes to get there and if there will be any delays on the day (market days, big

events, bad weather, etc. causing more traffic) and plan accordingly.

6. Make sure someone oversees the timings during the day and keeps the day moving, otherwise, you'll be doing your first dance at midnight.

7. The photographer will take ages and the caterer will need the meal to start on time.

8. The wedding breakfast will take about three hours. Trust me, especially if having a plated meal and interspersed with speeches.

9. The chances of the evening guests turning up during the speeches gets high the more relaxed a wedding you have. Hence the need for point 6.

10. Providing your own drinks and bar? Don't forget the corkscrew and bottle openers. And keep them tied to the bar area so they don't go walking. Seems obvious but easy to overlook (yes, it's happened).

11. Get referrals for your suppliers or vendors or check out review sites.

12. Wedding Insurance is essential – it doesn't cost much in the grand scheme of things.

I hope this book has given you plenty of insight into planning a wedding the wedding planner way and you can be confident that you won't miss anything during the planning process. If it does all get overwhelming, there are professionals available to take away the stress.

Good luck with the wedding planning and I hope you have an awesome wedding day!

Photo by Joe Stenson

ACKNOWLEDGEMENTS

"I don't wish to be everything to everyone, but I would like to be something to someone." — Javan

This book could not have happened without my amazing life coach, Alix Wilde (Holistic Leadership Coach), who gave me the insight to discover what was deep inside of me that needed to be expressed. With her guidance, probing questions, and wisdom, I found myself exploring new creative avenues and through those explorations, I found a door to the world of writing. And through that door, I realised I had all this knowledge that needed to be shared with the world. Alix, you are a gift to creatives and I am truly grateful for your wisdom and friendship.

To my amazing friend, my soul-sister, Angela, for being on my wavelength and introducing me to Alix in the first place. I met Angela when she booked me as her wedding planner about five years ago. Then fate brought us together again. Some friendships are just meant to be.

I also need to thank the contributors to this book who have allowed me to use their knowledge and words in some of the sections. Paula Brown, from Ollivision, an amazing photographer that I have worked with a number of times. Lee from Louisianna's Mobile Bar, for taking the time out of his busy schedule to talk to me. Natalie Willingham with her fabulous makeup advice and general wedding day tips. Becki and James from 2 Little Ducks

Videography, for their advice on videography and real-life stories, and Kath Lambert from the Wedding Flower Company, for her tips on choosing and working with a florist or venue stylist.

Obviously, I have to thank my husband, Neil, for putting up with me all these years. For coping with the kids when I was working at weddings most weekends during the summer. And for giving me the time and space to become the author I want to be. Love you, Babe!

I need to thank my copy editor Laura Wilkinson for her thorough editing and proof-reading.

And lastly, I have to thank all the wonderful couples who hired me as their wedding planner or on-the-day coordinator over the years. I have many wonderful memories and stories from your weddings and I wish you blessed and happy marriages.

CONTRIBUTORS

Paula Brown
Ollivision Photography
www.ollivision.co.uk

Louisianna's Mobile Bar Hire
www.louisiannas.com
lee@louisiannas.com

Natalie Willingham Makeup Artist
www.nataliewillingham.co.uk
@nataliewmakeup (twitter and instagram)

Becki and James
2 Little Ducks Wedding Videography
www.2-little-ducks.com

Kath Lambert Floral Consultant
www.theweddingflowercompany.net
kath@theweddingflowercompany.net

CHECKLISTS

Example Wedding Planning Timeline - 12 months to I do

Below is a list of the main things to do in the 12 months run up to your wedding day. Not everything will be relevant for your wedding.

12 months +
- Set the date
- Book the venue
- Give notice at local registrar office
- Draw up a guest list
- Book photographer
- Book videographer
- Book Wedding Planner or venue stylist
- Start wedding dress search
- Send save the date cards
- Book caterers
- Book Florist/Floral Designer

9-10 months before
- Book band and/or DJ
- Contact decor hire companies if you need to hire anything for your venue
- Book honeymoon
- Order the wedding cake
- Book transport - especially if wanting a vintage car
- Book musicians for the ceremony or drinks reception

6-8 months before
- Order your wedding dress - can take over 6 months to arrive, so do this

sooner rather than later
- Book honeymoon
- Check passports in date
- Plan hen and stag dos
- Book outside bar hire company if required

4-6 months before
- Choose invitations and other stationery
- Choose Grooms suit
- Hire formal wear for the men
- Choose bridesmaids dresses
- Make sure you have given notice (at least 3 months to your registrar or religious celebrant)
- Organise additional wedding transport (e.g. buses or coaches) if required
- Decide on floral arrangements and bouquets
- Arrange hair and make-up trials
- Collate addresses for your guests
- Research accommodation options to put in the invitations
- Set up gift list

2-3 months before
- Send out invitations
- Wedding dress fitting
- Buy wedding rings
- Choose gifts for the wedding party, parents, each other.
- Menu tasting with caterer
- Choose outfits for page boys or flower girls

- Make the place cards, or other DIY wedding items
- Run through information with your on the day coordinator

1 month before
- Contact all your suppliers to confirm details
- Final wedding dress fitting
- Finalise details for the ceremony
- Complete any wedding craft projects
- Contact any guests who have not replied
- Take some time out to relax

2 weeks before
- Give final numbers to the caterers and/or venue
- Create the table plan
- Give list of group photos to the photographer
- Pay final invoices to suppliers

1 week before
- Final run through with your wedding coordinator
- Create a timetable for the day and make sure all suppliers have a copy
- Create a list of supplier contact details including phone numbers to the person responsible for managing the day
- Pack your overnight bag
- Pack for the honeymoon
- Have your beauty treatment
- Full wedding dress rehearsal including underwear, veil and shoes to make sure it is all as it should be

2-3 days before

- Finalise the seating plan
- Grooms - finalise and collect all formal wear
- Confirm pick up time with transport
- Reconfirm with all suppliers
- Make sure people in your wedding party have a running order for the day including supplier details
- If having a marquee this should be erected and hired items can be delivered

Day before

- Drop off reception items (place cards, menus, table plan, favours etc) at the venue
- If you have a venue you can set up the day before then do this
- Make sure you have money in an envelope ready to pay any suppliers who need paying in cash on the day
- Wedding rehearsal with full wedding party at the ceremony location

Wedding day

- Make sure gifts are placed somewhere for easy access during the speeches
- Flowers will be delivered
- Wedding rings to the best man
- Assign a member of the wedding party to assist the photographer in knowing who is who for the group photos
- Enjoy yourself!

After the wedding day
- Rental items to be returned
- Wedding dress cleaning
- Send thank you notes to guests and vendors

Example Wedding Timeline

Time	Activity	Location
9.30	Make up	House
10.00	Wedding Coordinator arrives	Marquee
10.30	Hairdresser	House
10.30	Florist Arriving to drop off bouquets/buttonholes	House
11.00	Videographer arrives	House
11.00	Photographer arrives	House
11.15	Father of the groom collects buttonholes	House
12.00	Cake delivered	Marquee
12.00	Florist	Marquee
13.00	Bar arriving	Marquee
13.10	Groom and Groomsmen leave for ceremony	Hotel
13.30	Caterers arriving	Marquee
13.30	String Quartet arriving	Church
13.30	Car arriving	House
13.30	Groom and groomsmen arrive	Church
13.45	Leave for ceremony	House
14.00	Ceremony	Church
	Photographs	Church
14.30-15.00	DJ arriving	Marquee
15.15	Guests leave church	Church
15.30	Drinks reception on patio – bar serving in marquee	Marquee
	Canapes – caterers serving	Marquee
15.30	String quartet arriving – set up in marquee	Marquee
16.30	Guests seated in the marquee	Marquee
	String quartet playing	Marquee
16.40	Bride and Groom announced	Marquee
16.45	Speeches	Marquee
17.05-15	Food served DJ Playing	Marquee
18.00	Band arrives	Marquee
19.00	DJ playing	Marquee
19.30	Cutting cake and first dance	Marquee
20.15-21.00	Band First Set	Marquee
21.00	DJ back on	Marquee
21.00	Wedding Coordinator Finishes	Marquee
21.30-22.15	Band Second Set	Marquee
22.00	Evening Buffet	Marquee
22.15	DJ back on	Marquee
01.00	Finish	Marquee

Catering Checklist

So what do you need to think about when catering for your wedding?
- Does your venue already do the catering?
- Budget - how much per guest are you planning to spend?
- How many guests do you have?
- What are the catering facilities like at your chosen venue?
- What style of food are you going for?
- Can you go to a tasting session?
- Do they provide all the tableware? (including glassware)
- How many staff will they bring?
- How long do they need to set up?
- What equipment do they need? Are they supplying it or do you need to hire it for them?
- How long do they stay for?
- Do they take all their rubbish with them?
- Can they cater for food intolerances, special dietary requirements or allergies?

Marquee Checklist

These questions might be useful when choosing a marquee supplier:
- Are they available to do an on-site estimate?
- Will the marquee accommodate all your guests? Is there room to mingle? Is there room for a dance floor?
- What colour is the marquee? What types of lining are available?
- Is proper flooring available? What type?
- What about staging for speeches and entertainment?
- Do they also rent tables and chairs? Are they included in the price?
- Is there a sufficient power supply for any entertainment/sound systems you may require?
- Can the marquee hire provide a generator if additional electricity is needed?
- Can they provide interior lighting? Exterior lighting?
- Heating?
- A public address system for speeches/entertainment?
- Can your theme and decorations be incorporated into the structure easily?
- Is access to permanent shelter/house available?
- Can walkways be covered?
- Can the hire company arrange for portable toilets if necessary?
- How soon before the wedding day will they set up the marquee?
- When will it be dismantled?
- Will someone be available on-call during the event if there are any emergencies?
- How far in advance are bookings required?

- What is the cancellation/postponement policy?
- How much is the deposit to secure the date and when is it due?
- When is the balance due?
- Is VAT included in the final price?
- Confirm dates, times and details with a written contract.
- Get insurance.

Consultation Questions

These are some of the question prompts I used when talking to clients.
- Who is getting married?
- Who else do I need to know about?
- Estimated attendance numbers?
- What do you require me to do?
- When do you want the wedding to take place?

    What month?

    Weekday or weekend?

    Time of day?

    More than one day? (i.e can hire a hotel for a weekend)
- Where do you wish to get married? Distance from a particular city or town for example?
- What type of venue would you prefer? (Hotel, Countryside, City, Stately home, unusual venue, village hall, restaurant etc)
- Church, registry office or licenced venue?
- How long will the event last?
- How much is your budget?
- How do you plan to accommodate guests?
- Food (meal, buffet, canapés), drinks etc
- Will there be entertainment?

    What type?
- Do you have any specific requests? And ideas? Or themes you want to incorporate?
- What style of wedding? Formal, traditional, quirky, informal style
- Children present?
- Anything else?
- Photographer/Videographer?

Cutting the Cake and Cake Portions

Taken from http://bridalstudio.info/wedding-cake-servings/

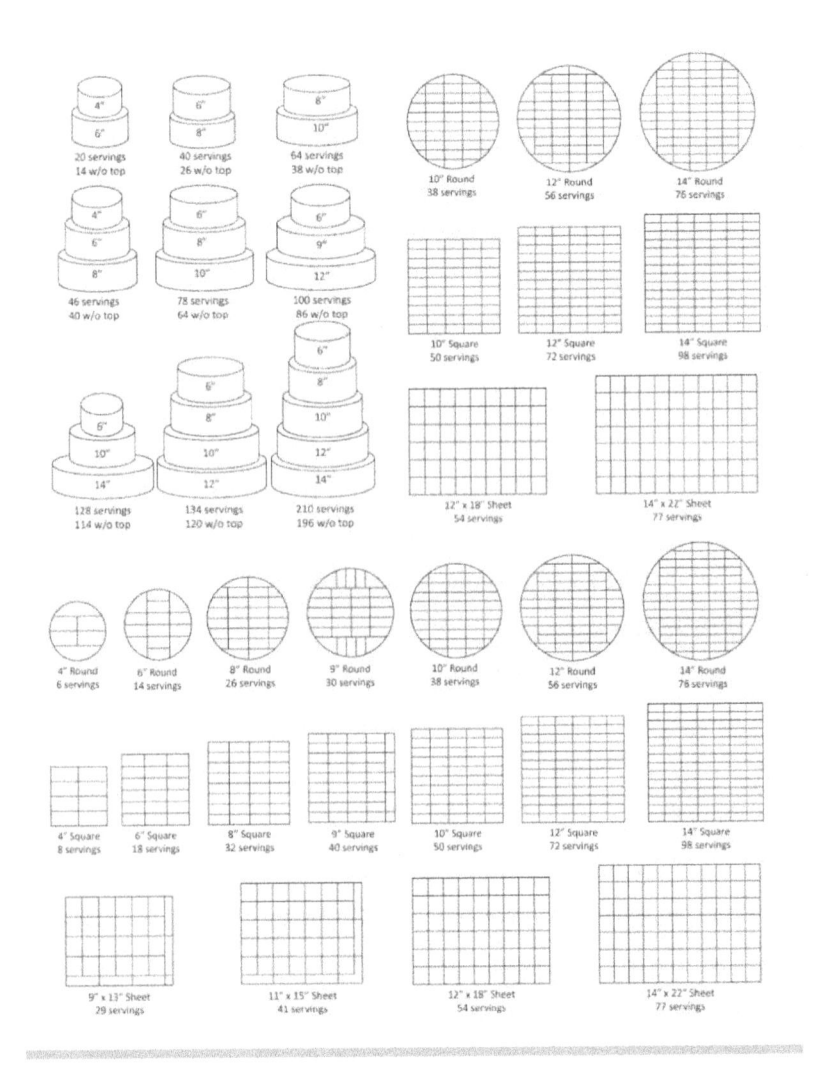

Tiered cakes:

- 4", 6" — 20 servings / 14 w/o top
- 6", 8" — 40 servings / 26 w/o top
- 8", 10" — 64 servings / 38 w/o top
- 4", 6", 8" — 46 servings / 40 w/o top
- 6", 8", 10" — 78 servings / 64 w/o top
- 6", 9", 12" — 100 servings / 86 w/o top
- 6", 8", 10", 14" — 128 servings / 114 w/o top
- 6", 8", 10", 12" — 134 servings / 120 w/o top
- 6", 8", 10", 12", 14" — 210 servings / 196 w/o top

Round:

- 4" Round — 6 servings
- 6" Round — 14 servings
- 8" Round — 26 servings
- 9" Round — 30 servings
- 10" Round — 38 servings
- 12" Round — 56 servings
- 14" Round — 78 servings

Square:

- 4" Square — 8 servings
- 6" Square — 18 servings
- 8" Square — 32 servings
- 9" Square — 40 servings
- 10" Square — 50 servings
- 12" Square — 72 servings
- 14" Square — 98 servings

Sheet:

- 9" x 13" Sheet — 29 servings
- 11" x 15" Sheet — 41 servings
- 12" x 18" Sheet — 54 servings
- 14" x 22" Sheet — 77 servings

Lightning Source UK Ltd.
Milton Keynes UK
UKHW021146271219
355981UK00015B/1174/P

Wedding Notes

some pretty paper and put in a large ornate frame.

Other ways I've seen is having a table with all the place cards on it in alphabetical order and the name card has the table number on.

A complicated but interesting version at one wedding had guest names in two columns down each side of the board. The tables were in the middle of the board and each name was attached to the relevant table with different coloured wool and pins! It looked really spectacular and complicated and obviously a lot of work had gone into it.

Pinterest will have lots of ideas. I'm not affiliated with Pinterest by the way - I just wish it was around when I was getting married! Instagram will also be a source of ideas.